Strategic Church Leadership

STRATEGIC
CHURCH
LEADERSHIP

*Robin Gill and
Derek Burke*

First published in Great Britain 1996
Society for Promoting Christian Knowledge
Holy Trinity Church
Marylebone Road
London NW1 4DU

Biblical quotations are from the *New International Version*, copyright © 1973, 1978,
1984 by the International Bible Society. Published by Hodder & Stoughton.

British Library Cataloguing-in-Publication Data
A catalogue record of this book is available from
the British Library

ISBN 0-281-04901-7

Typeset by David Gregson Associates
Printed in Great Britain by
The Cromwell Press, Melksham, Wiltshire

Contents

PREFACE

This book comes from the discovery that we had both been thinking independently about church leadership. The Church Commissioner investment losses and the continuing decline in church attendances worried us both. How should church leaders respond effectively to them?

Robin Gill's various studies of churchgoing decline in Britain had convinced him of the need for more creative thinking about strategic church leadership. Derek Burke's experience as Vice-Chancellor of the University of East Anglia had led him to believe that the skills of strategic leadership, managing rapid change effectively, were often absent from churches. Then, as a result of reading Robin Gill's article on subsidy in the *Church Times*, Derek Burke sent him a copy of the paper he recently gave to a Norwich Diocesan Conference.

After a meeting together we decided that a book was needed in this area, targeted specifically at church leaders It has been fun to do.

We are very conscious that a number of our friends and colleagues have helped us by reading earlier drafts. Mr Basil Collins, Mr Terry Cooke-Davies, Dr John Court, Dr Michael Northcott, Mr Derek Pearce, Bishop John Waine and Canon Robert Warren all read earlier drafts and were particularly helpful. Of course the views are finally ours and not necessarily theirs. Our two wives were, as always, supportive and constructive yet critical. To them all we offer our thanks, but to Jenny and Mary we offer our love as well.

INTRODUCTION

British churches – and especially the Church of England – are currently facing acute anxieties about leadership. The world seems to be changing fast and yet church leaders often seem perplexed and paralysed by change.

Churchgoing continues to decline in Britain. Yet church leaders are often reluctant even to admit this decline. There is a growing problem of authority and establishment. As an established church the Church of England faces many of the widespread criticisms that are made of other institutions, such as the monarchy and parliament, in Britain today. Yet church leaders are often at a loss to know how best to respond to this criticism. They face a paradoxical mixture of a growing secularism, of resurgent forms of fundamentalism, and of increasing religious pluralism.

Secure jobs are becoming for many laypeople a distant memory. Yet senior and junior clergy alike frequently insist that their jobs must remain secure, even while the very economic base of these jobs is becoming less and less certain. The Church Commissioners' investment debacle of the 1980s is likely to affect the Church of England for many years to come. Resentment is growing amongst congregations about the new financial burden arising from clergy stipends and pensions being increasingly placed upon them.

In short, church leaders in Britain at the moment are facing major problems.

We will argue in the course of this book that church leaders could learn much from the experience of leaders in other organizations facing similar rapid changes. Specifically, the concept of 'strategic leadership', which is proving so important in other institutions, is relevant to churches too and offers a more effective way of understanding leadership in a time of change. This concept is quite different from the understanding of church leadership that is often encountered. The latter sees consensus, harmony, balance, equality of distribution and historical maintenance as being the key features of good church leadership. In contrast, we will argue for ownership rather than consensus, for vision rather than harmony and balance, for priorities rather than equality of distribution, and for accountability rather than maintenance.

Of course strategic thinking, and management ideas generally, should not be adopted uncritically by church leaders. Churches are emphatically not businesses. They are *churches* and must be driven first and foremost by their commitment to God in Christ through the Spirit. Nevertheless we will argue in chapter 4 that strategic thinking, seen critically as a technique not as an ideology, does have significant insights to offer church leaders. There are even important theological connections that can be made. For example 'ownership' and 'accountability' are both profoundly theological concepts. The theme of owning visions occurs frequently in the Bible; a prophet or leader has a vision which he seeks to share with others so that they too may own it. The theme of grace is also crucial; each person is richly endowed by God with gifts to use in the service of Christ. It is not for people to boast about these gifts or visions but to accept them with gratitude in worship and then to use them responsibly, knowing that finally everyone is accountable before God (Mt. 25.31f).

The emphasis of the recent Turnbull Report upon the need for a clear theological base, for a strategic understanding of church leadership, and for central church structures which respond more readily to change, is most welcome. Members of the Commission that produced the Report are well aware that its proposals are but a first step in shaping the Church of England for the future. Our aim is to outline the second step. In the course of this book we will scrutinize a number of its recommendations for the Church of England, as well as its implications for other churches in Britain.

Since our own experience of leadership is largely in universities, it is from this world that we seek to draw parallels and to look for hints about how things might be done better in churches. We also believe that the changes facing modern universities offer the nearest parallels to those currently facing British churches. They are closer than those facing the business world or the National Health Service – although at times we will refer to some of those too. None of these changes are identical to

those facing churches. Once again, churches are *churches* . . .
they are not businesses or universities. Yet because churches still
need to be financed and organized effectively, especially in a
time of rapid social change, they do have some problems in
common.

Surprisingly there have been remarkably few recent studies
of church leadership and fewer still of strategic church leadership. We hope that this short study will provoke others to think
more deeply about the following question:

*How might church leaders today promote growth – qualitative as well as
quantitative – in the fast changing world of modern Britain?*

That is the central question in this book.

In the chapters that follow we will look first at church
leadership in the Acts of the Apostles, then at the rapid changes
facing any leader in the modern world, and only then will we
set out what is involved in strategic church leadership today.

CHAPTER ONE
Strategic Leadership in the Acts of the Apostles

There is nothing new about the issue of church leadership in a fast changing world. Indeed there are some rather obvious parallels with the situation facing the earliest Christians in the New Testament, with the Acts of the Apostles offering a remarkably strategic understanding of church leadership. We are very conscious that there have been many scholarly studies of this New Testament book – raising such issues as its dating, authorship, sources, theology, cultural context, as well as its relationship to the Pauline, semi-Pauline and Pastoral Epistles. None of these are our direct concern here. Rather more simply, whoever wrote Acts, from whatever sources and with whatever degree of historical and cultural accuracy, the opening chapters do still provide important insights into church leadership at a time of rapid social change.

Acts is very concerned with leadership. In the first chapter leadership is already a dominant theme. In the second verse the author recounts that before ascending, Jesus gave 'instructions through the Holy Spirit to the apostles he had chosen'. By the end of the chapter the eleven remaining apostles are busy electing a successor to Judas using a quotation from one of the Psalms: 'May another take his place of leadership' (1.20). Throughout the momentous changes facing early Christians, the focus of the first half of Acts is primarily upon the leadership of Peter (and sometimes Stephen and Philip), whereas that in the second half is upon the leadership of Paul. Even the sermons in Acts given by Peter, Stephen and Paul are typically structured around accounts of God's actions in the Old Testament focused upon leaders such as Abraham, Moses, David and Solomon.

Leadership in rapidly changing times is a dominant theme in Acts. What then are the key features of this leadership? There are eight which seem particularly important in Acts: together these features form the basis of a specifically *strategic* under-standing of church leadership.

First, church leadership is intimately connected with *worship*. Key decisions and key visions for leadership typically come out of a context of worship. Mission and social action both seem to flow from worship. Before the election of Matthias in the first chapter 'they all joined together constantly in prayer' (1.14). The dramatic second chapter opens with the words: 'When the day of Pentecost came, they were all together in one place' (2.1). Worship then leads them to a revolutionary empower-ment. At the end of the same chapter we are told: 'They devoted themselves to the apostles' teaching and to the fellow-ship, to the breaking of bread and to prayer' (2.42). From this worship flowed many wonders and signs as well as their com-munal giving to those in need. Thus 'they broke bread in their homes and ate together with glad and sincere hearts, praising God and enjoying the favour of all the people' (2.46–47). And so the pattern continues in the chapters that follow in Acts.

We will argue later that worship is still central to the life of the churches. However in modern Britain, a society that once worshipped is fast becoming a society in which only the few worship. What is for Christians the most normal of activities is becoming strange and alien to a growing part of the popula-tion. In the Acts of the Apostles worship is fundamental for church leadership.

A second feature is *vision*. Vision typically springs from prayer and worship. There is the dramatic vision of Stephen at the end of chapter 7, just before he was stoned to death: 'I see heaven open and the Son of Man standing at the right hand of God' (7.56). Having had this vision Stephen is able to pray 'Lord Jesus receive my spirit' (7.59), even as he was being stoned. There is the vision of Philip in chapter 8 prompting him to meet the Ethiopian eunuch. There is the momentous vision of Saul in chapter 9 on the road to Damascus: 'Saul, Saul, why do you persecute me?' (9.4). Following this vision Saul becomes 'my chosen instrument to carry my name before the Gentiles and their kings and before the people of Israel' (9.15). And then in chapter 10 there is Peter's extraordinary vision of strange and forbidden foods. First he 'went up on the roof to pray' (10.9), then he had his vision.

The third feature follows directly from this. A vision typically precedes a new and powerful sense of *priorities*. Saul's vision totally changes his life. The fervent persecutor becomes the ardent evangelist. Philip's vision leads to his encounter with the Ethiopian. Peter's vision leads him to reassess his understanding of who should be allowed to come to be baptized. Finally he concludes: 'I now realise how true it is that God does not show favouritism but accepts men from every nation who fear him and do what is right' (10.34). He now believes that Jesus Christ 'is Lord of all' (10.36).

Throughout this book we will stress that a clear sense of priorities based upon vision is essential for strategic leadership. Strategic leaders do not attempt to do everything; they are deliberately selective. Nor do they simply react to one event after another without any clear sense of priorities. On the contrary, strategic leadership is always focused.

Fourth, leadership is associated in Acts with an ability to spot genuine *opportunities*, distinguishing carefully between opportunities and *threats*. In chapter 8 the Ethiopian eunuch presents Philip with a real opportunity to preach 'the good news about Jesus' (8.35). Having been baptized by Philip after their discussion of a passage from Isaiah, 'he went on his way rejoicing' (8.39). In other words, Philip spots that this is someone genuinely struggling with Christian faith who can be led gently to see more. This is a real opportunity.

In contrast, Simon the sorcerer is finally unmasked as being a sinister threat. After practising sorcery for some time, Simon is baptized. He then 'followed Philip everywhere, astonished by the great signs and miracles he saw' (8.13). However, witnessing the work of Peter and John brings out some rather baser motives in Simon: 'When Simon saw that the Spirit was given at the laying on of the apostles' hands, he offered them money and said: "Give me also this ability so that everyone on whom I lay my hands may receive the Holy Spirit"' (8.18–19). Peter responds directly: 'May your money perish with you, because you thought you could buy the gift of God with money! You have no part or share in this ministry because your heart is not right before God' (8.20–21). Spotting genuine opportunities, as well as identifying potential threats, are both key features of strategic leadership.

This leads to the fifth feature in Acts – having identified

genuine opportunities leadership is carefully *selected* for defined tasks. Two instances of this feature are the selection of Matthias in chapter 1 and the selection of the seven deacons in chapter 6. The reason given for the selection for Matthias in the prayer at the end of chapter 1 is: 'Lord, you know everyone's heart. Show us which of these two you have chosen to take over this apostolic ministry' (1.24). Whereas the reason given for the selection of the seven deacons is even more specific:

> It would not be right for us to neglect the ministry of the word of God in order to wait at tables. Brothers, choose seven men from among you who are known to be full of the Spirit and wisdom. We will turn this responsibility over to them and will give our attention to prayer and the ministry of the word (6.2–4).

So, the author of Acts suggests, Stephen and the other six deacons were chosen to exercise pastoral care of the Grecian or perhaps Greek-speaking widows, while the twelve apostles devoted their attention to prayer and to preaching (and this despite the fact that Stephen is immediately shown to be preaching himself). Selection and role differentiation are both associated with leadership.

It is often imagined that church leadership should avoid all conflict. The good church leader should raise no hackles either within the churches or outside them. A church leader should be a healer of differences – a figure of consensus for Christians and non-Christians alike. Indeed church leaders can easily assume that their chief task is to be loved by everyone. The next two features of leadership in Acts suggest otherwise.

The sixth and seventh features are concerned with *conflict* and *ownership* – conflict between church leaders and the world at large and conflict and ownership within the early church and even amongst church leaders themselves. Conflict is so often feared in churches today and yet is so evident in the early Church. It requires a little more attention than the other features.

Being prepared to face conflict and even to recognize that it cannot always be resolved is one of the most enduring features of leadership in Acts. Of course this does not mean that church leaders in Acts set out to be hated. On the contrary they demonstrate in their lives many instances, small and large, of

7

compassion, care and love. At several crucial points they respond to the marginalized in society and their preaching resonates with the love of God shown to the world in Jesus Christ. Rather, being loved by others at the expense of avoiding conflict is not a priority of strategic leadership. Sometimes leaders, if they are to be effective in difficult situations, have to recognize that a degree of conflict is inevitable.

Repeatedly in Acts church leaders face bitter and protracted criticism from society at large. In chapter 2 those empowered by the Holy Spirit at Pentecost are immediately ridiculed by some of the bystanders: 'They have had too much wine' (2.13). In chapter 4 Peter and John are jailed by the priests and the captain of the Temple, since 'they were greatly disturbed because the apostles were teaching the people and proclaiming in Jesus the resurrection of the dead' (4.2). Twice Peter and John are hauled before the Sanhedrin, but they remain undaunted. On the first occasion, 'filled with the Holy Spirit', Peter announces:

> Rulers and elders of the people! If we are being called to account today for an act of kindness shown to a cripple and are asked how he was healed, then know this, you and everyone else in Israel: It is by the name of Jesus Christ of Nazareth, whom you crucified but whom God raised from the dead, that this man stands before you completely healed (4.8–10).

Despite threats, Peter is equally unafraid of direct conflict in his second inquisition before the Sanhedrin: 'Judge for yourselves whether it is right in God's sight to obey you rather than God. For we cannot help speaking about what we have seen and heard' (4.19–20).

In the next chapter of Acts Peter, together with the other apostles, is back in jail and is taken again before the Sanhedrin. Their defiance continues unabated:

> We must obey God rather than men! The God of our fathers raised Jesus from the dead – whom you had killed by hanging him on a tree. God exalted him to his own right hand as Prince and Saviour that he might give repentance and forgiveness of sins to Israel (5.29–31).

Members of the Sanhedrin are so angry at this that they want

'to put them to death' (5.33). Instead, on Gamaliel's interven-
tion, they are flogged and ordered 'not to speak in the name of
Jesus' (5.40). They, in turn, of course have no intention of obey-
ing this order. Not surprisingly, then, in chapter 8 Stephen is
stoned to death after his speech to the Sanhedrin. Yet even this
act is followed by open defiance by other Christians: 'On that
day a great persecution broke out against the church of
Jerusalem, and all except the apostles were scattered throughout Judea and Samaria . . . Those who had been scattered
preached the word wherever they went' (8.1, 4).

Defiance and a resolute preparedness to face outside conflict,
followed frequently by persecution, are themes that recur
regularly throughout the rest of Acts. Strategic church leadership must be ready to face conflict in the world and must be
prepared not to give way to it. Unfortunately the desire to be
loved runs very strong amongst many church leaders today. So
often they are passive, limited to responding to events, avoiding
extremes and keeping consensus going. The Acts of the
Apostles suggests rather that the existence of conflict does not
in itself denote failure. It might at times actually be a sign of
vitality.

Strategic church leadership also has to face conflict within
the churches. It is remarkable how frank the author of Acts is
about conflict, some of it never resolved, amongst the earliest
Christians. The hints that Paul's epistles give about internal
conflict within the early Church (for example in the opening
chapter of 1 Corinthians), are amply corroborated by the early
chapters of Acts. The extraordinary story of Ananias and
Sapphira in chapter 5 shows this clearly. Peter confronts them
both sharply. And then in chapter 11 it is Peter himself who
is confronted for baptizing Gentiles: 'The Apostles and the
brothers throughout Judea heard that the Gentiles also had
received the word of God. So when Peter went to Jerusalem,
the circumcised believers criticised him and said, "You went
into the house of uncircumcised men and ate with them"'
(11.1–3).

Although the author of Acts says that 'no further objections'
(11.18) are raised once Peter gives his explanation, by chapter
15 the issue clearly is not resolved. And even when the issue of
circumcision is apparently settled, there still remains some
unresolved conflict amongst church leaders. Barnabas appar-

ently wishes to take John Mark with Paul and himself. Paul, on the other hand, does not. Finally 'they had such a sharp disagreement that they parted company' (15.39) and, quite literally they go their separate ways.

Without assuming that internal conflict is actually desirable, it may be a mark of mature leadership to recognize that it will sometimes occur, especially amongst people with a determined mission. Precisely because strategic leadership involves vision and the setting of distinctive, obtainable priorities, individuals are likely to clash with each other. In contrast, if consensus and harmony become the major objectives for leaders, then it will not matter that particular visions and priorities are set to one side. What strategic leaders seek is *ownership* rather than consensus. They do not arrive empty-handed looking for meagre points of consensus amongst otherwise conflicting parties. Rather they arrive with a vision which they offer to others to shape, and then to own, for themselves. Unlike consensus leaders, strategic leaders are prepared to face conflict from those who finally cannot or will not own their vision.

The eighth feature of leadership in Acts is concerned with *outcomes* and *accountability*. It is quite common to hear sermons denouncing church statistics. 'What have numbers to do with the kingdom of God?' or, 'The number of people who go to church is irrelevant to the gospel of Christ.' Sometimes David's sin of numbering the Israelites (2 Samuel 24) is, rather quaintly, used as evidence to support this position. The author of Acts, however, seems to be surprisingly interested in numbers.

The first chapter of Acts mentions in passing that 'Peter stood up among the believers (a group numbering about a hundred and twenty)' (1.15). The next chapter states that after Peter's sermon at Pentecost 'about three thousand were added to their number that day' (2.41). And the end of that chapter says that 'the Lord added to their number daily those who were being saved' (2.47). By chapter 4 'the number of men grew to about five thousand' (4.4) and by the next chapter members of the Sanhedrin are complaining that 'you have filled Jerusalem with your teaching' (5.28). And, after Saul's conversion in chapter 9, the author of Acts writes: 'Then the church throughout Judea, Galilee and Samaria enjoyed a time of peace. It was strengthened and encouraged by the Holy Spirit, it grew in numbers, living in the fear of the Lord' (9.31). Of course, outcomes are not simply about numbers. In any case, who knows or will ever know how the author of Acts arrived at the specific numbers given in the text. Yet numbers are nevertheless an outcome which does seem to be significant to the writer of Acts.

In the context of over a century of churchgoing decline in Britain, we too believe that numbers are important. We will argue later that both a quantitative and qualitative concern about churchgoing should be a major priority for British church leaders today. Strategic leadership does make an attempt, wherever possible, to measure and assess outcomes against stated objectives as accurately and as truthfully as possible. A frequent sign of ineffective leadership is a tendency either to ignore or to excuse actual outcomes and accountability. Audit is an essential tool of strategic leadership.

In the course of this book we will examine each of these features of strategic church leadership portrayed in Acts – worship, vision, priorities, opportunities/threats, selection, conflicts both external and internal, ownership, and finally outcomes/accountability. They do still need to be taken very seriously by church leaders – especially at a time of rapid social change.

CHAPTER TWO
Coming to Terms with Change

> A crowd came together in bewilderment, because each one heard them speaking in his own language. Utterly amazed they asked: 'Are not all these men who are speaking Galileans? Then how is it that each of us hears them in his own native language? Parthians, Medes and Elamites; residents of Mesopotamia, Judea and Cappadocia, Pontus and Asia, Phrygia and Pamphylia, Egypt and the parts of Libya near Cyrene; visitors from Rome (both Jews and converts to Judaism); Cretans and Arabs – we hear them declaring the wonders of God in our own tongues!' Amazed and perplexed, they asked one another; 'What does this mean?' Some, however, made fun of them and said, 'They have had too much wine.' (Acts 2.6–12)

There was a time when the British welcomed change. The end of the Second World War was followed by a period of great social and political change – the Beveridge Report, which laid the foundations of the Welfare State, the Butler reforms to education, and State ownership of primary industries. There was a mood of optimism – the world could only get better. But now many no longer welcome change; it is usually accompanied by smaller budgets, job losses and greatly increased work loads for those still with jobs. Naturally people feel threatened, resist change, and finally become bitter and disillusioned.

In contrast, strategic leaders are learning how to deal with change. First in businesses, then in the universities, and now, this book argues, in the churches. The quotation from the Acts of the Apostles at the head of this chapter shows the early Church also faced considerable change. Change seems to be inescapable, as the Turnbull Report recognizes so well. Not to resist all change, nor to pretend it is not happening, but to deal with it strategically – that is what is important.

What does strategic leadership mean? Quite simply it means

taking the change that affects us all, and channelling it so that it takes us in the way we want to go. Of course change can be unwelcome and often unpleasant; it forces people to make difficult – sometimes very difficult – decisions; but crucially it must not be allowed to blow them off course. And to avoid being blown off course, people must know where they want to go. That is what strategic leadership means – steering a rational path through change to take people in the direction that best fits their values and vision. And because everyone is subjected to some of the same forces of change, and because there are similarities between institutions – universities and churches amongst them – we hope that our experience in universities can be useful to churches as they face a changing world.

But first, why should there be any change at all? Why cannot the world stay the way it was twenty, thirty or forty years ago? Why cannot things be left alone? Simply because this is a period of change as profound as the Industrial Revolution, driven by world-wide and deep-seated changes in the way the world works.

The Second World War left the industrialized powers with a virtual monopoly of technology, sources of capital, the means by which to conduct trade, information channels and the creation of popular culture. Europe and America had unrestricted access to cheap raw materials. The economic strength of the industrialized powers was taken for granted and individuals enjoyed a higher standard of living than ever before. But now all that is under threat. Tens of millions now have access to skills which were once restricted to tens of thousands. Skills and capabilities are spread far more evenly around the world than they used to be. Changes have taken place that are unlikely ever to be reversed, and the future of the Western World lies increasingly in the knowledge-based industries.

WHAT SORT OF CHANGES ARE TAKING PLACE?

There are obvious political changes – deep-seated changes whose outcome cannot yet be predicted. The older generation grew up in a period of political stability – the Cold War – but of tremendous personal suffering resulting from twentieth-century forms of totalitarianism; the forced collectivization of the 1930s in Russia, the Holocaust of the 1940s in occupied Europe, the sufferings of Eastern Europe in the 1950s and 1960s, the appalling sufferings in China in the so-called Great Leap Forward. Many rejoiced when the walls fell, but then soon became disillusioned. Bosnia, Serbia, Georgia, the Ukraine, and Russia itself, are not places of peace, stability or prosperity. Desperately people today try to stabilize them, wondering in the meantime what is going to happen in the Sudan, Algeria, South Africa and many other places. The price of freedom is, indeed, constant vigilance – as another Burke said two hundred years ago.

What has gone wrong? Many things of course, but one underlying theme is the growth of tribalism – an identification with, and allegiance to, a group smaller than the nation-state. People in the West are privileged; they can have many allegiances, or to put it another way, they can belong to many tribes – church, community, profession, country, Western democracy, and so on. They have the wealth and the stability to enjoy multiple allegiances. But if you are a Muslim in Bosnia, you belong to only one tribe and, if that tribe is threatened with extinction, you fight for your tribe, for otherwise you have nothing left. Complex political structures are proving very fragile.

But even in a stable, advanced democracy, such as the United Kingdom, separate allegiances are developing. Many would say that their nationality is Scottish or Welsh rather than British. Policy at the national level is increasingly influenced by well organized pressure groups targeting a single issue. This fragmentation of the nation-state has been accompanied by a demand for the devolution of power within the State. People apparently want more say in what affects them, possibly in regional assemblies, and there is much less confidence in central decision making bodies.

Then there are economic changes – equally deep-seated and long-lasting. The question, at its boldest, is whether and how, in this small island at the edge of a trading group, the British are going to maintain their standard of living. Not just to get richer – though that is the goal that all politicians seek to achieve – but to generate enough wealth to support the supply of those goods and services British people take as essential for 'civilized' life.

Why be so concerned about this? First, because of the huge growth in the world of the number of people who can provide cheap, skilled labour. In other words, people who will compete with Western Europe for scarce resources and who will work for much lower wages. Second, living in a global economy, few companies now make decisions on a national basis.

Three brief examples can be given: the first within Europe, the others outside. Derek Burke was recently trying to persuade a major British multi-national to support an able younger scientist, who was doing research of considerable importance to them, to stay in Britain rather than return to Germany. They were not interested. They said that they could access his work just as easily there as here; it was of no concern to them whether he stayed in Britain or not. A second example is from Southeast Asia. The company that manufactures the mouse – that essential animal for personal computers – is moving its manufacture from Korea to Indonesia because its labour costs in Korea are too high. A third example is that a key part of British Airways' reservations and ticketing function is now carried out by staff located in India, because wages for software engineers are lower there and these engineers are just as good as those in the West.

So how is Europe to maintain a manufacturing base as the world splits into three trading blocks – Southeast Asia, the Americas and Europe? Of course lowering wages for unskilled or semi-skilled work is one way of reducing costs to keep the West competitive. It is a way that the United States is using to force down their costs, but it is not likely to be acceptable in Europe. The French retreated from a direct attempt to lower wages below the legal minimum for the young. But it is happening indirectly in Britain; many of the new jobs that are being created are part-time and carry no benefits. Low-skill jobs – routine production line jobs for instance – are either being transferred abroad or are being replaced by robots.

However, the major recent change here has been the loss of many jobs in middle and lower management in large companies. This is partly due to the use of information technology to replace clerical and supervisory work. For example, Norwich Union which used to be able to recruit, every year, the majority of the school leavers from Norwich, is unlikely ever to do so again. Indeed, the size of that company will surely continue to shrink. ICI was turned from loss to profit in the 1980s by removing whole layers of management – 'delayering' is the jargon – and nobody really noticed. People who distributed information around the company, passing it up and down the line, or who read reports that others like them had written, were found not to be essential. BT, British Gas, the major clearing banks, have all been shedding jobs rapidly as they thin out and simplify their management structures – indeed they have to do so to stay in business. The tragedy is more about not creating enough new jobs, rather than failing to preserve old jobs.

For example, a manager and two others runs a factory making the electronic switch for car air-bags. They are working three shifts, seven days a week. This man and the two others manage it all. In the recent past there used to be another layer of three managers, one for each shift, but they have gone. Peter Moore, of the Institute of Directors, put it graphically on Radio Four: 'The economy is growing at 2 to 3 per cent, but productivity at 5 to 6 per cent; the difference is the loss of jobs.' And, of course, the 5 to 6 per cent is driven by industry's need to compete.

These economic changes, with all of their inherent moral ambiguity, are having permanent effects on the pattern of employment. The older style of working for the same company for thirty or forty years has largely gone – most people will now change jobs four or five times in their careers, often needing re-training for the new task. Charles Handy has an interesting calculation in his book *The Age of Unreason*, pointing out that people used to work about 100,000 hours in their working lifetime. This was made up by working 47 hours a week, 47 weeks a year, for 47 years – in all 103,000 hours. The new pattern is about half that – about 50,000 hours in a lifetime. But the new pattern will not be made up by working 37 hours a week for 37 weeks and 37 years. Rather, the 50,000 hours will be made up by moving in and out of work, with time out for education, training or parenthood, periods of part-time work and early retirement. Fewer than half of all jobs will be full-time by the year 2000. One new pattern will be 45 hours a week, 45 weeks a year, for 25 years (early retirement). Another, 25 hours a week for 45 weeks, for 45 years (part-time), or 45 hours a week for 25 weeks, for 45 years (temporary).

Organizations will change too. Companies such as BT, IBM or the major clearing banks are only staying in business by drastically altering their strategy and style, with many job losses. New ways of running large organizations are being developed. The customer-provider principle is making major changes to the way that the National Health Service or British Rail are being run. In both cases, the changes are being driven by a desire to bring costs down and to persuade people to look at cheaper or more efficient ways of running an organisation by using an internal market. Everyone is involved in buying or selling and, in that way, watching costs rather than letting someone else 'up there' deal with costs. It is too soon to be certain yet how well it is working, but it has become imperative to find a way of containing the costs of such large organizations and also, and this is very important, maintaining the motivation and morale of those who work for them.

It turns out that there are many different ways of running business organizations. It may be totally dispersed, for example, with everyone working at home but connected by information technology. Then there is what Charles Handy, again in his book *The Age of Unreason*, calls the 'shamrock organization' – a company made up of three parts – a small, highly-paid core of permanent senior managers, a second made up of temporary workers, and a third of work contracted out to small independent companies. The company can readily expand or contract to meet market needs. Or there is the federal organization, where the decisions are made at the periphery of the organization, with the centre maintaining a strategic and financial overview (which is how multi-nationals work); or organizations which demand a great deal of consultation – for example the universities and indeed the churches – where there is again much decentralization but a stronger sense of the institution and where consultation, debate and often tension, precede decisions. The old-style company with its multiple layers and strong reporting lines, with information flowing up and decisions coming down, turns out to be a poor way to handle change.

All of this puts huge strain on leaders and workers at every level. In industry senior managers are judged by how well they steer their company through continuing change. Carrying out the old job is not enough. How successful they are in doing the new job is the key question. So they work very long hours, 60 to 70 hours a week, and have to meet high expectations. This imposes great strains upon workers too; people cannot be sure that their jobs are secure; all have to assume that jobs will continue to change. As a result, few people in the work place feel secure and, because of this and because economic expectations have not fallen, few families now can rely on a single wage-earner.

That one shift is related to many other changes, including some of the changes in the relative roles of men and women in Western society. Employment shifts from a full-time predominantly male workforce to an increasingly part-time female workforce. More men in the process become unemployed and marginal to household budgets. It is not too surprising that marriages suffer, that economically self-sufficient women can see less and less advantages in marriage, and that young unemployed males find that security in either employment or in relationships is ever more elusive.

Another transforming force is information technology. The phone, the fax, the telephone answering machine, the personal computer, the personal organizer, are now part of many daily lives. Electronic mail, remote access to data sets – for example library catalogues – are coming into daily use. And children are already at five and six years old being given computers for their birthday presents. Technology is changing the way people work and also the way they use their leisure time. Shopping by fax followed by home delivery is already in use in North America. Shopping by remote access – either by viewing the objects on television screens at home, or by a tour, using virtual reality, through a non-existent supermarket – are in sight. Banking can now be done by telephone and fax and many of the day-to-day transactions that fill up people's lives can be transferred to electronic media.

But there is a more profound way in which information flow – whether through education or the media – has changed many lives. Western societies are now increasingly made up of educated people who prefer to choose for themselves. Indeed, education is now available world-wide, with high levels of skills being possessed by millions of people. An unprecedented amount of information is also available: many people see access to information as a right, and hierarchies, accustomed in the past to operate by managing the information flow, today find it hard to retain their authority. Élites everywhere have to justify their roles; they are no longer closed. Skills too are global and finance is global. Management and administrative skills are no longer the preserve of a Western white élite. Anyone can manage, anywhere in the world.

Beyond and underneath these changes lie profound social changes. Weakening of authority, rejection of Christian values, a mixed-faith and non-faith society, a fundamental change in the role of women, rapidly changing attitudes to marriage, and many other cultural changes. Christians seem to be powerless to influence changes which are often viewed with deep dismay. Indeed, we often cannot agree among ourselves as to what should be done, and so we become defensive and depressed.

Yet these changes, however unwelcome, will not easily be reversed. We are certainly not claiming that all of these large social and cultural changes should be welcomed with open arms by church leaders. Some should quite properly be resisted. However most are with us whether we like it or not. Nostalgia for a society that has gone – and that includes the full employment security of the 1950s – is largely irrelevant.

Nor will these changes stop. It is not as though people have had to make a once-and-for-all adjustment to changed but now static circumstances, but rather that they have to adjust to living with continuous change. The company that survived the early 1980s found that the world of the late 1980s had moved on, and so it had to change again to meet the challenge of the early 1990s, and so on. There is no Shangri-La just around the next turning where people can stop and rest – only a process of continuous change.

Few church leaders have come to terms with this yet.

RESPONDING TO CHANGE

The easiest response is not to notice that it has happened, to pretend that it has not happened, or even to assume that it will all soon blow over. Few of the companies that reacted in this way in the 1980s are here any longer – whether they were small family-owned businesses, long-established businesses, well-known chains, or large national companies.

Another way to respond is to wait for rescue from outside – help from Government, the European Union, or another company. The universal lesson seems to be that this strategy only buys time. Occasionally, but rarely, that was enough, but something else had to happen. That something else was a change in the way things were done, not superficial mechanization changes like installing a new computer, but deep-seated attitude changes. A change in culture, no less.

Many of Britain's institutions are going through such changes – industry, the Civil Service, the National Health Service, the research councils and the universities. It is the thesis of this book that British churches face such a change, and that there are lessons to be drawn from these examples and specifically from the universities. For there are some similarities between churches and universities. Universities are often, like churches, ancient institutions with a history of which they can be proud. Like churches, universities are staffed by bright, independent people who do not accept the authority of others readily. Like churches, universities are conservative in style and liable to self-pity. Like churches, universities are often rather unaware of how much the world outside has changed. Such similarities are obvious. Yet universities have been changing fast for a decade now – so perhaps there are some lessons from our experience that may be of help to churches. The Turnbull Report is certainly convinced about the need for such change. The authors regard their radical changes as both 'essential' and ' urgent', maintaining that 'uncertainty will damage staff morale' (*Working as One Body: The Report of the Archbishops' Commission on the Organisation of the Church of England*, 1995, para. 4.20).

The similarities extend further for universities have, like churches, been losing resources ever since the 1973 oil crisis and especially rapidly over the last decade. For example, grant and tuition fees per student in universities, the income for all teaching, have fallen by almost a quarter over the last five years alone. Similar changes are occurring in the Church of England with the loss of capital by the Church Commissioners and a consequent loss of income. Leaders in both institutions need to deal strategically with these financial problems.

Universities have, again like churches, had morale problems. University staff have often felt undervalued. Change can seem to call into question what they have been doing in their work for many years. Since their effectiveness in this work depends so heavily upon inner motivation, a crisis in morale is particularly damaging. For such people, whose drive comes largely from within, the outcome can be disastrous. There are clear similarities here once again with churches. Leaders in both institutions must deal with these morale and motivation problems. And neither universities nor churches have always been able to agree a common policy. For fifteen years universities have been so busy competing with each other and arguing internally that one of their essential joint functions – namely negotiating effectively with Government – was lost. Too much energy and time was spent by university leaders attempting to resolve their differences. In the churches, too, arguments over internal issues, sometimes only marginal to a mission to the world at large, can all too easily consume precious time and energy. Just think how long it took to resolve the issue of women priests in the Church of England and how much longer it might take to resolve that of homosexuality.

Universities have faced and still face major changes. Churches are currently facing some very similar changes. But so does each person as an individual. Most people have had to cope with rapid change in their own lives. The amazing technological changes of the twentieth century alone have ensured that. There are some individuals in the world who have managed to avoid twentieth-century technology out of choice, but they are few and far between. In reality, many people within cultures which are denied advanced technology are only too keen to claim the benefits of this technology – whether in the form of transport, communication or entertainment. One anthropologist noted dryly that only those who have always had matches to light fires and metal saws and axes to chop down trees denounce all of the fruits of modern technology. Indeed, part of our ecological problem as we enter the new millennium is precisely that most of us find advanced technology only too seductive. An ability to change rapidly in this area is a part of our daily experience.

Just think, for example, about the rapid changes in health care provision over the last century. In the initial phases of a health care strategy, pure water, good sanitation, clean, dry housing, and a healthy diet are priorities. Once these are provided for most people in a country then life expectancy will increase dramatically. However after this the quality, if not the length, of life can be further enhanced by medical technology – and few people wish to be denied the benefits of this technology. And this is despite the fact that medical technology can carry with it some bleaker side-effects. It is, after all, medical technology which allows us to keep the irreversibly comatose 'alive' and which enables us to use invasive procedures on the terminally ill. The fruits of modern medical technology are not unambiguously beneficial, but they are none the less in ever greater popular demand.

Again consider computers. Some people, including some church leaders, argue that computers tend to produce a privatized world of screen watchers who have lost many of the skills of social communication. Children nurtured on a mixture of television, video games and computers will – so it is argued – increasingly confuse fiction with reality, withdrawing into a fantasy world of their own. They will fail to develop skills of conversation and social interaction and their bodies will suffer from lack of exercise. In addition they will be unable to write properly, to do much mental arithmetic, or even (given the existence of spell and grammar-checks on many computers) to construct coherent, literary English unaided. Prose for them will consist of semi-literate memos. And the adults nurtured by this process will never have learned some of the most basic skills of cultured life. The word processor makes writing just too easy and too functional. An ability to write eloquent books will have been lost.

Of course there is some force in these criticisms. There are dangers in the computer revolution, but it is fanciful to imagine that it can be treated as a passing phase. Even those who make such criticisms are often adept at using cash-dispensers as well as the computer catalogue in libraries. The reality is that the computer revolution is here to stay. There is also something slightly odd about the cultural criticisms of computers that are often made. All of the objections to television and computers just listed could in a previous century have been used against book reading. It too encourages the privatization of leisure time, it too might detract from social skills and physical exercise, and it too might mislead people into confusing fantasy with reality.

Perhaps all that is being said is that every generation has a tendency to be suspicious of the technological and cultural changes of the next. Yet, despite such suspicion, everyone lives inescapably in the same world. An older generation might be more reluctant to respond positively to rapid change, yet it does respond. Colleagues, well into retirement, become adept at computer skills; the electronic information highway is open to young and old alike.

It is important not to be uncritical of change and not to treat all change as 'progress'. Cultures seem both to learn and to unlearn. Every generation, for example, tends to be critical of the sexual and family relationships of the previous generation. Yet there is little evidence to suggest that sexual and family relationships actually improve from one generation to another. Again, in an ecologically fragile world many people are less confident today that all of the recent technological changes are actually sustainable. For example, there is good reason to be deeply worried about the effects on the atmosphere of emissions from ever multiplying cars. While change cannot be avoided altogether, people do need to remain vigilant about some of the harmful effects of change.

Exactly – the way people respond to rapid technological change in their individual lives is with a mixture of acceptance and vigilance. People become adept at coping with rapid change effectively and creatively even while voicing criticisms. They can see the obvious benefits of modern technology, even while they tend to view it with a mixture of fear and suspicion. And they are able to do this because they can distinguish benefits from side effects. They can see the advantages that technological change brings to their lives even if they are also aware of some of its disadvantages. In short, rapid change forces people to decide upon priorities – that is, to think strategically.

It is possible to approach institutional change in a similar way. It could be, although this is rather unlikely, that institutions such as churches and universities have no need to change at all. They are already perfectly suited to the world. Yet that world is changing and changing fast. And those of us who lead secular institutions realize that we have to lead them through continuing change if our institutions are to survive. We are convinced that church leaders face similar challenges. They too could deal strategically with change in the same way as have university and business leaders, and as people do as individuals, with a mixture of acceptance and vigilance. Change can become an opportunity if people know where they want to go.

As Charles Handy says, the *status quo* is not an option.

CHAPTER THREE
What Has Gone Wrong?

After we had been there a number of days, a prophet named Agabus came down from Judea. Coming over to us, he took Paul's belt, tied his own hands and feet with it and said, 'The Holy Spirit says, "In this way the people of Jerusalem will bind the owner of this belt and will hand him over to the Gentiles."' When we heard this, we and the people there pleaded with Paul not to go up to Jerusalem. Then Paul answered, 'Why are you weeping and breaking my heart? I am ready not only to be bound, but also to die in Jerusalem for the name of the Lord Jesus.' When he would not be dissuaded, we gave up and said, 'The Lord's will be done.' (Acts 21.10–14)

PROBLEMS FOR THE UNIVERSITIES

Over the last ten years or so, the universities have changed almost out of recognition: a doubling in the number of universities; a threefold increase in the number of students; a change in the nature of the student population, with many more mature and part-time students; a constant fall in the amount of money per student; increased competition between universities; and a staff–student ratio which has almost doubled.

What has brought about these changes? How have university leaders responded? Are there lessons here for church leaders? Perhaps the latter might cope with change rather better than Paul's colleagues in the quotation at the head of this chapter.

The root causes for the university changes lie in two major social and political changes: the first is the urgent need to increase the number of university graduates and the second the increasing pressures on budgets. Traditionally, Britain only educated a small proportion of its 18 to 21-year-olds in universities: only 8 to 10 per cent even after the large expansion of the 1960s and much lower before that. Young people were often trained through apprenticeship, for example to engineers, or by being articled, for example to solicitors. Education was not the route out of the immigrant community or a lower social class that it was in North America (and partly in Scotland), and was generally less highly valued. The British universities were restricted originally, of course, to training for ordinands and the learned professions such as medicine and law. But wave after wave of expansion and change has altered that.

To the two ancient universities of England and the four of Scotland were added, in the nineteenth century, many new universities. Durham was founded in the 1830s, quickly followed by the first colleges of the University of London, and then, in the second half of the nineteenth century by the universities of the great industrial cities. In the early twentieth century came the development of more colleges of the University of London, the campus universities of the 1960s, and now the doubling of the total number of universities in the early 1990s. An education system that was developed to serve the learned professions and to train a ruling élite for a major trading nation at the centre of a large Empire is no longer sufficient to meet the needs of the late twentieth century. Now it is the knowledge-based industries whose development is crucial for Britain's future. The expansion had to come, and Britain has now just about caught up with the United States and Japan in the proportion of our population in tertiary education.

The expansion was inevitable and it had to be paid for – by a nation whose income was rising only slowly and in which there were major competing claims, for instance from the National Health Service. As a result, costs per student have been driven down. Indeed, most universities have been losing resources at 3 to 4 per cent per year for ten years now, and will continue to do so for the foreseeable future.

How have the universities and their leaders reacted? Derek Burke went as Vice-Chancellor to the University of East Anglia in January 1987, when the University was facing a 17 per cent cut over three years. The initial reactions were typical of the system as a whole. The University had already weathered a series of cuts in the early-middle 1980s and now thought those times were past. So, understandably, the first reaction to the new cuts was stunned anger – 'How dare they do this to us?' and 'The Barbarians are at the gates.' It was unconstructive, terrible public relations and was easily interpreted as arrogance. Indeed, there was some arrogance, but for others it was genuine disbelief – 'Surely everyone realizes the supreme value of the British universities?' That was the trouble – they did not. So the major problem was a disjunction of values inside and outside the universities. The universities were sure that they were more valuable than the rest of the population, which had itself been through wrenching, difficult years. An obvious lesson here for the churches.

The next reaction from academics at the University of East Anglia was that someone would rescue them – like the end of an old Western film, the US Cavalry would gallop in. So confident were they of such a rescue that some seriously proposed that universities should continue to spend, run up deficits and wait for Government to bale them out. Again, all that showed was how unaware they were of how society had changed. Such overspending meant, of course, running a deficit – something which universities are able to do and which may be quite proper in certain circumstances. But a deficit year after year? 'Well', said the temporizers, 'let's use the reserves and stop repairing the buildings, anything but losing jobs.' But most universities had small reserves – only enough to cover a year or two's overspend. Unfortunately, working in buildings where the roof leaks is no long-term solution.

All of these short-term solutions were ways of avoiding the real crunch – that the overall income was just too small to keep everyone employed, especially in a situation where over 70 per cent of the annual budget went on salaries. So, reluctantly, it was accepted that jobs would have to be lost. But how?

The first move of university leaders was to freeze all vacancies – not just as a short-term stop-gap measure but indefinitely. This is a useful way of bringing home to an institution how serious the problem is, but since vacancies occur at random, this action would very quickly create a crisis. Key parts of the University of East Anglia would soon have been without vital workers, while less crucial parts would have remained undisturbed. Very quickly the pressure to release some posts for refilling would have become unstoppable, and some would have had to be refilled. But which? How can the institution decide which posts are really essential? In the absence of an overall strategy it is an impossible task. The winners would usually be those who shout loudest or those with the most power.

So people decided that cuts really did have to be made. But by whom, and where? How does a collegial institution, unused to making difficult decisions, and whose style is to attempt to please everyone, make such decisions? The easiest answer is for leaders to avoid making any decisions at all and to go for equal misery all round. So everyone is cut back equally. But this assumes that everyone is equally important and that everyone can survive. These assumptions simply are not true, of course, but what is even more serious is the effect on morale and motivation. It is natural for everyone to conclude that the institution is inexorably running down – 5 per cent this year, 5 per cent next and so on until just a rump is left. People then see nothing to work for. There appears nothing that they can do to save the institution. It has no future and the best course for them is to leave.

These are the reactions of an institution that refuses to face questions about its future. Such a lack of clear decision making stems from confused objectives, lack of priorities and absence of vision for the future. The issue was also compounded by years of incremental budgeting, in which allowances for inflation had been added year by year without any questions being asked about whether the final distribution actually made sense. We will return to this crucial issue in chapter 6.

It is the job of strategic leadership to bring the institution to make difficult decisions and to make them in time. Realistic decisions can only be made when institutional priorities are clear and agreed – and that is why strategic planning is needed. Decisions also need to be made in time; not so late that the institution is exhausted, financially and in every other way. Otherwise there is no energy left for change. History, especially recent history, is littered with the hulks of institutions that were too late in seeing what they had to do. Their leaders failed them. Church leaders must not do the same.

PROBLEMS FOR THE CHURCHES

British churches share with universities both of the root causes of recent change – namely, an urgent need to increase numbers and growing pressures on budgets. Perhaps church leaders could learn from some of the mistakes and successes of those involved in dealing with change in the university world. Numbers and budgets are inescapably a part of these two worlds. Strategic leadership offers a way for both to cope rationally with these changing numbers and budgets.

In neither case are these central objectives. It would, of course, be disastrous for either the universities or the churches simply to increase numbers and budgets while failing altogether to attain their mission objectives. Just imagine for a moment a university which ignored its mission to achieve excellence in teaching and research and decided instead to sell its degrees for a bargain fee and for only a token amount of student work. It might well enrol plenty of students and show a healthy financial balance, but it would soon become an object of ridicule amongst other universities. We will come to the mission objectives of churches in the next chapter, but just imagine a church that decided to abandon Christian worship which taught and moulded as many people and structures as deeply as possible and, instead, decided to offer only populist activities aimed at gathering in the masses as profitably as possible. It too would soon become an object of ridicule.

Numbers and budgets clearly should not become central objectives in either universities or churches. They are the *raison d'être* of neither. And those universities or churches in which they do become central objectives are rightly not to be taken seriously. Nevertheless both universities and churches do still have to get numbers and budgets right. If either finally fails to attract sufficient numbers and continuously runs a deficit budget, it will eventually cease to function.

Colleagues in both the universities and churches sometimes protest that things are otherwise. There are still some university academics who decry all links between student numbers and budgets. 'What have these to do with real scholarship?' And there are also some clergy who disclaim any links between numbers of churchgoers and budgets. 'The size and giving of congregations should not determine whether they have paid clergy.' We are thoroughly familiar with both of these reactions and fully understand their passion. Yet, in the end, if no such links are made, these institutions will simply collapse and protesting colleagues will be without their salaries. Numbers and budgets are not central objectives for either churches or universities. They are just minimum conditions for achieving their respective mission objectives. If there are insufficient numbers or funds, central objectives cannot adequately be met.

Of course there are also real differences lying behind these similarities. The most obvious of these concerns numbers. The last few decades have seen a growing student demand for places in British universities and the funds coming with these new students have been crucial in balancing their budgets. Yet there has been no corresponding popular demand for church membership. Quite the contrary. There is now overwhelming evidence that overall churchgoing and church membership across denominations has been declining throughout the twentieth century, both in Britain and in many parts of Europe.

Robin Gill has documented this decline at considerable length in *The Myth of the Empty Church* (1993), so it is unnecessary to rehearse it in full here. The outline, however, is clear. Whereas in 1851 approximately four out of ten of the adult population of England and Wales were in church or chapel on an average Sunday and most attended on an occasional basis, by the 1990s it is little more than a third of the adult population that attends on an occasional basis and only a tenth that attends on an average Sunday. There has been a long slow decline in churchgoing which has seen few interruptions. For more than a century, decade by decade, fewer adults worship in churches in Britain.

Churchgoing in urban Anglican churches started to decline in about the 1850s. Free Church churchgoing gradually overtook Anglicans in many cities until about the 1870s, and probably kept *overall* levels of urban churchgoing relatively static at approximately four out of ten adults on an average Sunday. However from that point onwards Free Church churchgoing also started to decline, bringing about the almost uninterrupted pattern of overall churchgoing decline. Beginning from a much smaller base, the Roman Catholic Church slowly increased attendances, until the late 1960s when it too started a sharp decline. The one in ten adults currently in a church or chapel on an average Sunday are now divided fairly evenly between Anglican, Roman Catholic and Free Churches. Despite evidence of increasing membership and attendance in some Evangelical/Charismatic Churches since the 1970s, as well as a few well-publicized recent Anglican transfers to the Roman Catholic Church, *overall* churchgoing and membership continue to decline.

This decline is something that both of us deeply regret. We take no pleasure in stating it so bluntly. There have been many attempts by church leaders to gloss over churchgoing decline and even the Turnbull Report, despite its boldness in other areas, makes no mention of this decline. Some have claimed that there is evidence that decline has recently halted or even reversed. Minor changes in annual figures sometimes encourage this view. Others have expressed doubt about whether there really has been such a continuous process of decline at all. Yet, however understandable, such reactions are still misguided. The evidence of overall decline in attendances (and in membership in those churches which have a concept of membership) is well documented and overwhelming. Unless it is acknowledged frankly by church leaders, there is little hope that they will be able to deal effectively with change.

The same principle applies to church finances. A frank acknowledgement of past financial limitations and mistakes is a prerequisite of strategic leadership in the churches today. Since the late nineteenth century there has been a grave financial problem at the heart of many British churches. While churches were still buoyant and expanding, huge amounts of private wealth – often new industrial wealth – was given to them. Places like Barrow-in-Furness, rising from a village in the 1840s to a vibrant industrial town in the 1880s, received large amounts of this private wealth. During that time the Free Churches turned a predominantly Anglican village into a Free Church town by building numerous Methodist and other Free Church chapels. Newcomers to the growing town brought with them both money and energy to achieve this. Anglicans, in turn, responded by building four identical churches, with a seating capacity of nearly six hundred people each and financed almost entirely by the nobility and by the share-holders of the shipyard. A similar pattern can be found all over

England. The Free Churches vigorously and competitively built chapels using the money of both local people and new-comers, while Anglicans built their churches in response and largely with outside finance.

However by the end of the nineteenth century this vigour began to wane sharply. Many of the Free Churches faced massive debts. Frankly, in many areas they had overbuilt. Encouraged by a huge population growth, by urban expansion and by new industrial wealth in the earlier parts of the nine-teenth century, they had considerably overstretched themselves by the end of the century. Then population growth, urbaniza-tion and industrial development all started to slow down and expansionist churches began to face serious financial difficul-ties. They had built church buildings and chapels speculatively throughout the nineteenth century, but by the end of the century these buildings typically were only a third full on an average Sunday.

The results became quickly apparent. About one hundred years ago many churches almost achieved their target of having a presence in every community with an ordained minister resident within it. The Anglican Church came nearest to meet-ing this target. Many small country parishes which had not had a resident priest since the Middle Ages now had their own incumbent. Rural tithes were revived (sometime after extended court cases), urban churches were built and endowed, new dioceses were created and endowed, and at last it seemed that an effective ministry could be offered to every community. On average there was at least one ordained minister and a church or chapel of one denomination or another for every thousand people in the country. Today, however, the number of ordained ministers has more than halved, rural ministers of any denomination typically look after at least three churches, and more than half of the Free Church chapels have closed. In rural areas Anglican churches increasingly are the only churches still open and they often struggle to remain so. In many rural and city-centre areas the sheer cost of maintaining ancient parish churches with dwindling congregations becomes an all-consuming task.

And now the massive investment losses of the Church Commissioners have added considerably to this burden. The lack of their financial control in the 1980s has been acknowledged very frankly by the Lambeth Report and now by the Turnbull Report. Yet it is important to note that these particular losses are not the *cause* of the Church of England's financial problems. These causes are of much longer standing. A reliance upon subsidy has been a feature for at least two hundred years. The vigour of church building in the nineteenth century was largely made possible by generous patrons. Unlike the Free Churches, few Anglican congregations financed the building of their church or the payment of their clergy themselves. Indeed, once a church and its endowment was established, it made no financial difference to an Anglican incumbent whether or not he had an effective congregation. He received his salary, and latterly his pension, regardless. In contrast, a Free Church minister's livelihood was typically dependent upon his congregation.

Precisely because the Church of England has been so heavily dependent upon invested income for the maintenance of its clergy, the effects of the Church Commissioner losses are now seen as nothing short of catastrophic. Whereas British universities and the Free Churches have faced a gradual erosion of their finances over the years, the Church of England, in contrast, faces a sudden and massive financial loss. Many of its traditional activities appear overnight to have become unsustainable. As the Turnbull Report again acknowledges, astonishingly in a time of actuarial change, not even clergy pensions were adequately protected by the Church Commissioners.

However, we will argue in the course of this book that there are actually some benefits in this situation and from local churches becoming self-funding. Reliance upon subsidy for day-to-day activities has severely stunted the possibility of growth for the Church of England. Paradoxically it seems also to have contributed to the demise of the Free Churches. Given the availability of the occasional offices of a national church at very little cost to them, it has always been difficult for most of those people who are nominally religious to see why they should contribute to the Free Churches.

There are theological reasons for believing that it is *self-funding churches* that are preferable. Just before the First World War, the remarkably far sighted missionary Roland Allen noted that:

St Paul not only did not receive financial aid from his converts, he did not take financial support to his converts. That
it could be so never seems to have suggested itself to his
mind. Every province, if not every Church, was financially
independent. The Galatians are exhorted to support their
teachers (Gal. 6.6). Every Church is instructed to maintain its
poor. There is not a hint from beginning to end of the Acts
and Epistles of any one Church depending upon another,
with the single exception of the collection for the poor saints
at Jerusalem . . . St Paul observed the rule that every Church
should administer its own funds. He certainly never adminis-
tered any local funds himself. (*Missionary Methods: St Paul's and
Ours*, London, 1912, pp. 73 and 84)

Allen went on to argue that Victorian missions overseas had
been hindered rather than helped by being so heavily subsidized. Instead of teaching local churches to be self-funding,
well-meaning missionaries in effect had encouraged them to
become dependent upon money and clergy from Britain. As a
result, he believed, local congregations in mission churches
tended to lack vigour and initiative.

The recent House of Commons Social Security Committee's
report, *The Operation of Pension Funds: The Church Commissioners
and the Church of England Pensions*, argued that the Church
Commissioners' losses may have a drastic effect upon clergy
and parishes for years to come. They stated bluntly:

We encountered a certain degree of complacency about the
loss of up to £800 million of the Commissioners' capital
base. Even if Sir Michael Colman and his new team at the
Commissioners are successful, there still remains a substantial risk that the Church of England could be transformed
out of all recognition: pension increases may be more
limited in the future than they have been; the number of full
time priests is likely to fall; the parish system will receive less
financial support from the Commissioners' resources;
churches, the centre of many local communities, will be lost
as parishes are amalgamated and practically all of these
closures will occur in the poorest areas of the country.

All of these represent drastic changes for the Church of
England as a direct result of its financial losses. These are not

just 'paper losses' due to a temporary drop in the property market. A significant proportion of the losses are likely to be permanent with direct implications for the day-to-day life of the Church of England.

Members of the committee were also just as blunt about the reasons for this huge loss of capital base:

> According to the evidence we have received, over the period from the mid 1980s to 1992 the leadership of the Church Commissioners: failed to comply with normal accounting practices that are a legal requirement in the commercial world, thereby creating a misleading impression of the true state of the Church's finances; established a series of development companies into which major injections of funds from the historic resources of the Church of England were made without due diligence; allowed the Archbishop of Canterbury only to learn fully of the financial losses by reading the Financial Times; foolishly speculated without proper expertise or advice in property developments using borrowed money; irreparably damaged the income flow to the Church jeopardising any future attempts to raise both the meagre stipends of clergy and still more importantly to be able to add significantly to the real value of their pensions; published misleading information in their annual reports on the value of their portfolio; has in all likelihood done more than any other single act to destroy the parish system of the national church; and failed to take steps to assess and meet greatly increased pension obligations.

Two factors are paramount in this situation: a dangerous dependence upon subsidy and inadequate strategic control and accountability. The Church Commissioners were not driven by greed, as has been alleged so often in the Press. Rather they felt themselves under considerable pressure to supply the Church of England with as much investment profits as possible simply to allow it to sustain its existing ministry. Despite real increases in congregational giving over the last few decades, the continuous decline of churchgoers, increasing bureaucratization in dioceses, and a growing number of clergy on pensions, have all made heavy financial demands upon the Church Commissioners. If they had been successful their investments might, it was hoped, have produced the income necessary to maintain the *status quo*. After successful property speculations in the 1970s and early 1980s, it is not too difficult to see why some of the Commissioners were tempted to increase such speculations in the late 1980s and early 1990s. Nevertheless the results, in terms of their own objectives, have been disastrous.

The other factor is surely inadequate strategic control and accountability. The House of Commons committee repeatedly pointed to this. Property speculations were made secretively, ill-advisedly and they lacked serious audit. Even today after all the various reports on their activities, it is still exceedingly difficult to unravel the details of all of the Church Commissioners' property speculations. It was not simply that the Church Commissioners were caught like many other institutions by the property collapse. It was that, compared with those responsible for large pension funds, they behaved secretively, unaccountably and in ways lacking in professional management. Perhaps this illustrates a wider malaise within many British churches. The inadequate strategic control of the Church Commissioners was invisible to so many church leaders precisely because the latter seemed largely unaware of the considerable fund of modern knowledge about strategic leadership in other institutions. Ironically, many businesses now have much higher standards of public accountability.

In short, if church leaders had looked to the modern university or business worlds during the same period of time, they might have seen how finances and strategy could have been managed more effectively and accountably in a similar context of rapid change.

CHAPTER FOUR
Setting Priorities

From Miletus, Paul sent to Ephesus for the elders of the church. When they arrived he said to them: 'You know how I lived the whole time I was with you, from the first day I came into the province of Asia. I served the Lord with great humility and with tears, although I was severely tested by the plots of the people. You know that I have not hesitated to preach anything that would be helpful to you but have taught you publicly and from house to house. I have declared to both Jews and Greeks that they must turn to God in repentance and have faith in our Lord Jesus Christ. And now, compelled by the Spirit, I am going to Jerusalem, not knowing what will happen to me there. I only know that in every city the Holy Spirit warns me that prison and hardship are facing me. However, I consider my life worth nothing to me, if only I may finish the race and complete the task the Lord Jesus has given me – the task of testifying the gospel of God's grace.' (Acts 20.17–24)

We have argued that church leaders in modern Britain are inescapably involved in dealing with rapid change. They can choose to do this effectively and creatively, using the insights and experience of other leaders who work in fast changing secular institutions. Or they can ignore or dismiss as irrelevant such experiences and insights and cope with managing change as best they may in other ways. Yet change will not simply go away. The shifting economic base of churches, new patterns of professional employment and tenure, and the day-to-day work experiences of those in the pews, ensure that church leaders are inevitably confronted with the problems and challenges of rapid change within churches today.

In dealing strategically with rapid change in institutions a clear sense of priorities is a prerequisite – the sort of sense of priorities illustrated well in the above address from Acts of Paul to the Ephesian church elders. Frequently this can be difficult. Complex institutions today, containing conflicting agendas and interpretations and confronted by confusing and diverse changes in the world at large, do not readily generate clear priorities. The university world knows this only too well. Academics, who are trained to think independently, and are given a considerable amount of unstructured time in which to do their research, seldom find it easy to reach a consensus about their priorities. Yet, as a result both of government policy and of strategic leadership within universities, they do now have clear priorities. Excellence in teaching and research *are* their priorities. Everything else is subservient to these.

It sounds so easy. Excellence in teaching and research seem the obvious things that universities ought to do. To the outsider it might seem that these priorities could have been established with little argument. The reality has been quite otherwise. These are hard-won priorities, arising out of critical and sustained thought about what it is that universities attempt to do which makes them distinctive. Other institutions, particularly in industry, do research. Other institutions clearly teach. However it is *the* distinctive feature of universities that they seek to combine excellence in research with excellence in teaching. They assume that their teaching staff are typically also engaged in creative research and they allow them considerable space, compared with other teaching institutions, to enable them to do this.

Once this much is discovered about an institution, strategic planning and audit cycles become possible. But that is for later chapters. The focus in this chapter is upon priorities. Unless an institution and its leaders are clear about priorities, dealing with change effectively and creatively within it is difficult if not impossible. For both individuals and institutions a clear sense of priorities, linked to what are perceived as their main objectives, is essential when managing rapid change well.

This also applies to churches. Unless church leaders have a clear set of priorities, they cannot deal with rapid change effectively and creatively.

Of course there will be many in the churches who have serious misgivings about this claim. 'Management' and 'strategic planning' are not exactly popular words amongst all academics. They are even less popular amongst many doctors and nurses in the National Health Service – which has relied very heavily upon a form of strategic leadership and management seldom involving doctors or nurses directly. Professional journals in both of these areas frequently carry articles decrying what they see as the modern and pernicious 'ideology' of management. A constant complaint runs as follows: 'I did not become a doctor to end up as a manager' or 'I became an academic because I was enthralled with my subject, not because I wished to spend my time responding to management demands.'

Some of the hostile responses to the Turnbull Report have shown very similar reactions. One vicar retorted in the *Sunday Telegraph*: 'Well, it's just the Church of England plc now.' And Bishop Eric Kemp probably spoke for others when, at the end of an otherwise thoughtful critique of the Report, he stated:

> What the Commission says about staff should be carefully scrutinised. Phrases such as 'a single unified staff, developing a coherence and singleness of purpose', and 'staff must be given freedom to manage, and more responsibility and accountability for directing the outcome of their work', ring alarm bells about the approach of Sir Humphrey and the Civil Service. These things may be appropriate in the financial and business world. I doubt whether they are so over the whole range of the Church's life . . . In the end, the question is whether what is suitable and appropriate for a business organisation is equally suitable and appropriate for all aspects of the life of the Body of Christ. (*Church Times*, 17 November 1995)

The argument here derives its force from an assumption that 'management' and the business world are alien worlds to the Church.

Bishop Nigel McCulloch, who has been highly involved in the Decade of Evangelism, has also voiced criticisms of management ideas. His warnings are important because he has been a strong supporter of more business-like efficiency within the Church of England. His worries are not those of a reactionary who has never attempted to change:

> There is absolutely no doubting the fact that, in the increasingly difficult tasks clergy are facing, as much pastoral support as possible is needed. But I am not at all sure that

systematic appraisal and review is coterminous with good pastoral care. What deeply worries me is the way in which, often uncritically, we are adopting too many of the assumptions and techniques of modern management. That is not to deny that there are some good ideas from the secular world which the church could adapt, and indeed does, with advantage. But, increasingly I am persuaded that the proper context for reviewing and developing ministry ought not to be quasi-management but spiritual direction. Indeed, if appraisal and review are not chiefly a spiritual matter then something is wrong. Most problems in our church life and our personal life, whether we are lay or ordained, are spiritual problems. A good spiritual director will understand enough psychology to appreciate different personality traits – and be able to give wise advice, based not only on knowledge but his or her own depth of spirituality. Furthermore, a spiritual director is not going to put things on files – so, for clergy especially, there is a huge release and opportunity for frankness and honesty which are unlikely in a hierarchical, and even a peer, system. But, even more important, placing this firmly within spiritual direction avoids the growing problem of answerability to those who increasingly pay the stipend. The inevitable blunting of prophetic ministry and the narrowing of mission outreach is a very disturbing feature of certain free churches where the elders insist: 'we pay you – so you must do and say what we wish'. (*Wakefield Diocesan Newsletter: See-Link*, March 1995)

Now, it is true that management and strategic leadership theory adopted uncritically and thoughtlessly can indeed be extremely damaging. For example, teaching audits in universities, which concentrate exclusively upon techniques and ignore the actual substance of what is taught, can be deeply misleading. Amongst an increasing number of management theorists there is now a recognition that institutions can over-plan and become too rigid. Henry Mintzberg's striking book *The Rise and Fall of Strategic Planning* (Prentice Hall 1994) argues that institutions do need to remain flexible, to respond imaginatively to unexpected changes, and to be open to creative visions. Yet, having admitted that, techniques and planning should not simply be ignored. Effective teaching does have to

give some attention to such mundane issues as library resources, bibliographies, audibility, intelligibility to the listeners,
as well as to student feed-back and to review procedures.
Mintzberg himself concludes that 'too much planning may
lead us to chaos, but so too would too little, and more directly'
(p. 416).

Surely this is also true of churches. Leaving it all to 'spiritual
directors' is just insufficient. Of course theological and spiritual considerations should be the starting point for ministry
within churches. In the first chapter we make this abundantly
clear – arguing that the Acts of the Apostles is still a very appropriate resource to start a consideration of church leadership.
Yet theology is not the only resource for effective church
leadership.

In his presidential address to the new General Synod,
Archbishop George Carey made a very similar point:

> Loose talk about 'managerialism' is . . . very unhelpful. If a
> person cannot manage then he or she is not well equipped
> to be an effective priest or bishop. But, of course, being a
> manager is but a small part of being a leader in the Church.
> If it is not shaped and formed by spiritual vision it will be
> directionless . . . Sometimes I encounter . . . frustration in
> committees which are not as effective as they might be . . .
> holding the ring between different organisations or . . . trying
> to cope with problems which stem from our current
> incoherence. I long for the day when that substantial time
> commitment can be used more productively. (1 December
> 1995)

In a similar vein, the Turnbull Report is emphatic that
theology must be the driving force of change within churches:
'the chief resource of the Church is the grace of God. No
amount of structure and organisation can "put the Church
right" if, at every level, it is not turning to God for his provision'
(para. 2.19). Yet, while a theological agenda is crucial, it is not
exhaustive. It provides the direction in which ministry should
go, but it does not provide the means for checking whether or
not this has been achieved effectively, that is for monitoring
outcomes.

We will return to outcomes in chapter 8. For the moment,
it is important to stress that there *is* a role for audits and

appraisals – properly understood – within ministry which are indeed recorded and kept on file (but not, of course, on secret files). On its own spiritual direction might well ensure that individual ministers are properly motivated. What it will not ensure is that they are also effective and contributing creatively to the Church as a whole. What must, for example, a church with a declining budget keep and what must it let go? Spiritual direction as such will not help here, but a clear sense of priorities, firmly based upon theology, will. Once such a firm theological base is secured, techniques from strategic leadership do have significant insights to offer.

It is important to emphasize that these are techniques and not ideology. Of course strategic leadership and management theory can be turned into an ideology – and perhaps that is Bishop Nigel McCulloch's legitimate worry – but that emphatically is not our intention. Nor is it even the intention of the more sophisticated management theorists. Mintzberg sets out at great length the disasters that can befall institutions which adopt a slavish approach to strategic planning. Business leaders who treat strategic plans almost as if they are creeds soon come to believe that everything can be pre-determined, that all outcomes can be accurately forecast, and that forecasting is a form of 'magic'. Ironically such a credal approach to strategic planning was often adopted in the Soviet Union before 1989: 'they controlled everything in their plans except the weather. Nature intervened, the crops failed, and the plan was thrown into turmoil' (p. 239). Strategic leadership should properly be regarded as technique not as creed.

Perhaps the most telling sentences in the quotation from Bishop McCulloch are the last two. Yet only a heavily subsidized church could criticize the Free Churches, talking about 'the growing problem of answerability to those who increasingly pay the stipend'. We suggested in the previous chapter that subsidy has in fact deeply misled the Church of England. It has for long given some of its clergy the impression that they can be more 'prophetic' than Free Church ministers. In reality in the nineteenth century, when prophetic ministry was both common and effective (especially amongst socially conscious Evangelicals), it was some of the entrepreneurial Free Churches which were the more prophetic. The Church of England, by comparison, resolutely tended to defend the *status quo* on moral and political issues.

A thoughtless use of subsidy also allowed the Church of England to maintain church structures which contributed directly to numerical decline. Far from economic subsidy freeing the Church of England to engage in mission outreach, it tended to cushion many of its clergy from any impetus towards such outreach. In effect it allowed clergy to be paid whether or not they were engaged in mission outreach and whether or not they had effective congregations. In contrast, a clearer connection between payment and answerability has been an important factor allowing American churches to flourish while their British and European counterparts have tended to decline.

In the wake of the recent report of the House of Commons Social Security Committee on the Church Commissioner investment losses, a leader in *The Times* identified some of the key issues here:

> Financial responsibility must be properly devolved to individual parishes . . . Far too much income is redistributed from vibrant churches to lacklustre parishes which have grown used to external subsidy. A new balance must be struck, giving greater emphasis to local self-sufficiency. Parishes should have greater freedom to explore economies of scale, such as the more intensive use of church premises. Team ministries should become more common. Local business skills should be tapped. Competitive tendering should become standard practice when churches spend their funds. For the parish system to survive, it will have to become leaner. Some churches will close or will lose a resident vicar. But the sooner this process of change begins, the smaller will be the number that have to go . . . Anglicans must realise that there is no alternative to change of this kind. If this financial disaster prompts a collective resolve to address the problem, adversity will have been turned to good use. (21 April 1995)

There are many issues here to be explored in later chapters. However this quotation sets out rather more clearly than most church based statements the enormous challenge that faces British churches, and particularly the Church of England, at the moment.

MISSION STATEMENTS

This leads us to mission statements. If establishing clear priorities is an essential first step in leading an institution strategically in a time of rapid change, then a mission statement is an important way of achieving this.

Perhaps in more static times it was possible simply to continue practices from the past which had already proved productive. Each generation could simply imitate the previous generation, or at least imitate those practices of the previous generation which seemed to work. On this understanding, a profession is a learned body that has preserved and carried forward wisdom accumulated from the past. However, in times of rapid change, such an understanding becomes distinctly more problematic. Rapid change tends to make accumulated wisdom appear anachronistic. It disturbs established patterns and makes fresh thinking imperative. In short, it requires a clear sense of priorities, vision or 'mission'.

It is ironic that this theological term – 'mission' – has been so widely borrowed by strategic and management studies. There is now widespread discussion in many institutions about 'mission statements' and 'visions' with very little awareness that theological language is being borrowed. Perhaps it is time for the churches to repossess their theological terms, albeit with the strategic leadership sharpness still attached to them.

Mission statements are an attempt to capture the central priorities of an institution in a brief formula. They emphatically do not contain all of the aims and objectives of an institution, unless of course it really is a single function institution. Complex institutions, which have long histories and a diversity of people working within them and attached to them, will more typically contain a variety of competing objectives. These will vary both within time and across time. Nevertheless what a mission statement tries to do is encapsulate what it is that makes a particular institution distinctive. Ideally a mission statement should give an outsider an idea of how this particular institution is different from other institutions. It should give a clear indication of the primary objectives of a particular institution as it encounters a rapidly changing world. A mission statement should provide a focus – a focus both for those within the institution as well as for those outside that institution.

Mission statements should provide clarity. They should make it easier to distinguish the central priorities and objectives of an institution from its peripheral objectives.

What are the central priorities and objectives of churches in Britain today?

The danger is that a whole cluster of answers might be given to such a question. For some Christians various forms of social action will be priorities. The main objective of churches is to transform the structures of the world in a Christ-like direction, fighting against poverty, discrimination and social injustice. For others the central objective is rather to preach the gospel and to bring individual lives to Christ. For them evangelism is a main priority. For some it is pastoral care; for others it is preaching; for some it is prophetic witness; and for others again it is liturgy. Christians from different liturgical positions are likely to produce widely differing responses to this question. There is no obvious theological way of avoiding this. Sadly theology and liturgy divide churches as much as they might unite them. Over the past decade the Church of England, struggling with such issues as the ordination of women and lay presidency at the Eucharist, has become acutely aware that this is the case.

We propose to start the other way around. Rather than asking the question from an insider's perspective, it can be asked as a question that might be addressed to churches as they are set in modern, secular/pluralistic Britain. Specifically in this context, what might be seen as distinctive about churches today? In what crucial ways do they differ from the other institutions that surround them in modern Britain? What do they offer, believe and do which is special, even unique?

Surely one of the most distinctive features of churches in modern Britain is that almost alone they engage in and encourage worship. In the past it might have been assumed that most people worshipped at some point in their lives. At the turn of the century, for example, a majority of the population went to Sunday school, often on Sunday afternoon. They also went to a church school during the week. Even if most adults at that time went to church only occasionally, almost all had worshipped as children and might be expected to worship again if they joined the army, attended civil functions, or went to weddings and funerals. Regular children's worship and occasional adults' worship were the norm.

Today, however, the situation has radically changed. We have already noted the long and relentless decline in adult church-going; since the 1870s, decade by decade, fewer adults worship in churches in Britain. In contrast, the Sunday school movement grew throughout the nineteenth century and maintained a substantial following in the first half of the twentieth century. However, since the 1950s it too has declined very rapidly. By the year 2000 the percentage of children in church or Sunday school will probably be little different from the percentage of adults in church on an average Sunday (probably about 9 per cent). Furthermore, they will largely be the children of the adults in church.

This creates a new and disturbing religious map in Britain. Sunday school membership can be traced back to the early nineteenth century. Even then it accounted for only about a fifth of all children. Today with little more than a tenth of children having formal, regular contact with churches, most will have no direct experience of worship outside of school assemblies. In addition, there is now overwhelming evidence that new churchgoers have typically been to church or Sunday school as children: most are 'returning' to church rather than starting afresh. This has meant that congregations can success-fully recruit a proportion of their members from amongst those who did once go as children and who now face life-changes – such as having children themselves, or being confronted with illness, bereavement, or retirement. In the next generation such people may be few and far between. Most people will not 'return' to church as adults because they have never been there in the first place as children.

Not surprisingly, school assemblies themselves become increasingly difficult to sustain. Formal excuses are sometimes made for this by headteachers. There is no room large enough to accommodate the whole school for a traditional assembly. Or there are too many youngsters belonging to non-Christian religions. But, the reality is probably that worship in any form is an alien experience for most children, as well as for a growing number of school teachers. It might still be possible to teach *about* religious traditions to youngsters who have no direct experience themselves of growing up in a religious tradition. After all it was perfectly possible for a previous generation to be schooled in the language, culture and mythology of classical Greece and Rome. What becomes much more difficult to see is how a generation, which belongs actively to no religious tradition, can be expected to engage meaningfully in school worship. Young people today can no more do that than could the previous generation have engaged in classical polytheistic worship and animal sacrifice!

Churches, however, *are* still committed to corporate worship. Along with synagogues, mosques and temples, they are in this respect quite distinct in modern Britain. Religious Jews, Christians, Muslims and Sikhs go to great lengths to provide buildings for worship and ordained ministers to lead this worship. Within each of these monotheistic faiths, corporate and public worship is clearly a central priority. Indeed, we have already shown that it was a clear priority for the early church as depicted in the Acts of the Apostles. Yet in modern Britain worship is largely neglected. Public worship in schools, prisons, the armed services, and even on civil occasions, is increasingly becoming an option for the few not an experience of the many. Even though many people in modern Britain still claim to pray privately, at least on occasions, most no longer worship corporately.

One of the clear repercussions of this situation is evidence of a growing confusion amongst young people about religious and moral beliefs. Belief in after-life in general declines, but belief in reincarnation increases. Belief in God, and certainly in a personal God, declines amongst teenagers, but a purely secular, materialistic outlook also remains unpopular. Vegetarianism and concern about ecological issues increase, but moral norms are less and less derived from mainstream religious traditions. New Age literature increases, while Christian books are sold mainly to churchgoers. It would appear that a society that worships less and less is also a society which is more and more confused about what it believes and values.

Worship should form an important element in any mission statement for the churches. However, worship alone clearly does not distinguish churches from synagogues, mosques or temples. Rather the worship of mainstream churches is distinct because it is addressed to God in Christ through the Spirit. It has proved notoriously difficult in ecumenical bodies, such as the World Council of Churches, to find an expression of faith which might be affirmed by all those who describe themselves as Christians. That is not our intention here. Our focus is rather upon mainstream, trinitarian churches in modern Britain. By definition for them worship is of God in Christ through the Spirit. An adequate mission statement should clearly reflect this.

Such worship constitutes the core of our mission statement. This is, so to speak, the vertical feature. A horizontal feature is important too, since most churches also believe that they are committed to teaching and changing individuals as well as moulding social structures through Christian faith, morality and worship. This horizontal feature is double-edged: it is concerned with both outreach and with social action. Outreach is the attempt to draw outsiders into the church, whereas social action is the attempt to engage the church with the needs of the outside world.

These three features – worship, outreach and social action – constitute the building blocks for our mission statement for the mainstream churches in modern Britain. They are very close to the threefold mission of the local church envisaged by the Turnbull Report:

> Our response to God's graciousness is threefold – worship, service and witness. **Worship** is the response of the creature to the creator and without it our humanity is diminished. Christian worship is radically trinitarian. In the power of the Holy Spirit we respond to a God who has revealed himself – in creation, in history and supremely in the person of Jesus Christ . . . **Service** to the community is the second aspect of the Church of England's tripartite mission . . . Worship without active love in the world leads to spiritual ghettos. Jesus made it clear by his life and his teaching that worship, teaching and healing were integral to each other . . . Christians are required not only to care for each other but for anyone in need . . . **Witness** is the third element of the Church's mission . . . The disciples were to be witnesses to Jesus and to his resurrection (Acts 1.8, 22). The first apostles derived their authority by teaching what they had experienced and making new disciples . . . Witness implies holiness of living, teaching the faith and evangelism. (paras. 2.2–16).

Naturally these three features, however named, do not

exhaust *all* of the objectives and aims of these churches. Yet together they might constitute a core of objectives. Above all they might provide a clear vision for strategic planning within churches at a time of rapid social change.

Our suggestion for a mission statement is as follows:

The central aim of churches in modern Britain is the communal worship of God in Christ through the Spirit, teaching and moulding as many lives and structures as deeply as possible through this worship.

Christian worship, outreach and social action – or worship, witness and service if you prefer – are all fundamental to this mission statement. It also assumes that worship is *communal* and involves *teaching* and *moulding* – both the lives of *individuals* and the social *structures* within which they live. Over the chapters that follow we will attempt to unravel the implications of this mission statement for strategic church leadership in a time of rapid change.

CHAPTER FIVE
Determining Objectives: opportunities and threats

In the Introduction we identified eight features of strategic leadership in Acts – worship, vision, priorities, opportunities/ threats, selection, conflicts, ownership and finally outcomes/ accountability. Worship, vision and priorities are fundamental to our mission statement. Worship of God in Christ through the Spirit we see as the *raison d'être* of churches. It should be both their primary vision and their clear priority. Through this worship we believe that lives and structures can indeed be moulded and taught. In this present chapter we will set out some of the opportunities and threats facing churches as they seek to enact this vision and determine their objectives. In chapters to come we will look at some of its implications for selecting tasks, facing conflicts, sharing and owning visions, and assessing outcomes and increasing accountability.

OPPORTUNITIES AND THREATS IN ACTS

In the Acts of the Apostles the one who faces more threats than anyone else, and yet the one who consistently identifies opportunities despite or even through these threats, is Paul. The second half of Acts is largely an account of the growth of the early Church under the extraordinary leadership of Paul, constantly threatened by fellow Jews and hassled by those in power. For years scholars have debated to what extent the account of Paul in Acts can be squared with the Pauline letters elsewhere in the New Testament. Once again it is important to emphasize that this is not our concern here. Our focus is rather on the insights offered by the author of Acts into strategic church leadership in a context of rapid social change.

The account of Paul in Acts is rich in such insights about worship, vision, priorities and determining objectives when confronted with opportunities and threats. This can be illustrated by looking briefly at just three chapters in Acts, chapters 16 to 18. Early in chapter 16, Paul has a crucial vision:

> During the night Paul had a vision of a man of Macedonia standing and begging him, 'Come over to Macedonia and help us.' After Paul had seen the vision, we got ready at once to leave for Macedonia, concluding that God had called us to preach the gospel to them. (16.9–10)

The vision of the man of Macedonia presents Paul with a clear opportunity – as well as a great deal of threat – for preaching the gospel both to Gentiles and to Jews living in a Gentile world. On reaching Philippi he and the author of Acts (the famous 'we' in this quotation seems to include the author of Acts for the first time in the narrative) look for a place of worship and meet Lydia. Soon she and her household are baptized.

Their next encounter is more threatening. On their way again to a place of worship, they meet a slave girl 'who had a spirit by which she predicted the future' (16.16). She taunts Paul and his companions for several days before he responds. However, since her owners have made a great deal of money out of her predictive skills, they are understandably furious with Paul and Silas for ridding her of this spirit. The owners publicly accuse them before the magistrates of 'throwing our city into an uproar by advocating customs unlawful for us Romans to accept or practise' (16.20–21). Sent to jail as a result of this charge, Paul nevertheless takes the opportunity to preach to and baptize both the jailer and his household.

In the next chapter Paul looks for fresh opportunities of sharing his faith, in Thessalonica, in Berea, and then in Athens. In each of these places he goes to the synagogue 'as his custom was' on the sabbath. Worship is always depicted as being central to his ministry. And in each place there is strong reaction to his teaching. In Thessalonica and Berea the crowd 'rounded up some bad characters from the market-place, formed a mob and started a riot in the city' (17.5). Paul's reception in Athens appears more ambiguous. In response to his celebrated sermon to a meeting of the Areopagus 'some of them sneered', but others responded: 'we want to hear you again on this subject' (17.32).

The Athens sermon itself well illustrates the four initial features of leadership. It starts with an observation about an object of worship and with a conjecture about the vision of the Athenians behind this object: 'what you worship as something unknown I am going to proclaim to you' (17.23). Paul uses this as an opportunity for directing the Athenians' worship to God made known in Christ. This theme is the sermon's priority. Driven by worship and vision, this sermon identifies a clear opportunity. In short, as a sermon it provides an ideal model of church leadership.

In chapter 18 Paul is in Corinth. The same four features of leadership are also evident here. Every sabbath 'he reasoned in the synagogue, trying to persuade Jews and Greeks' (18.4) and it is here that he has another crucial vision: 'One night the Lord spoke to Paul in a vision: "Do not be afraid; keep on speaking, do not be silent. For I am with you, and no-one is going to attack and harm you, because I have many people in this city"' (18.9–10). As a result of this vision, his new priority becomes clear: he 'stayed for a year and a half, teaching them the word of God' (18.11). Whereas in some places Paul discovers only threats and consequently leaves quickly, here he sees realizable opportunities and remains for a considerable period. And, having stayed with his fellow Jews and tentmakers, Aquila and Priscilla, he finally sets sail with them for Syria, travelling from place to place and 'strengthening all the disciples' (18.23). By now the couple have come to share and to own Paul's vision. At the end of chapter 18, it is they rather than Paul himself who are explaining the Christian faith to the learned Jew, Apollos. They too can now identify opportunities and discern threats when determining their objectives.

OPPORTUNITIES AND THREATS TODAY

What are the opportunities and threats facing British churches today as they seek to determine their main objectives? In order to identify them quite a number of different church groups have already discovered the merits of doing a SWOT analysis. Many Anglican parishes were encouraged to analyse their situation more carefully as a result of the report *Faith in the City* and have continued to do so in response to the Decade of

Evangelism. SWOT analysis has proved to be particularly popular.

This form of analysis derives its name from identifying four key features of any organization – its strengths, weaknesses, opportunities and threats. The language of SWOT analysis has begun to enter congregational life – often through lay people who use it regularly in their work. For them it is no longer an alien, secular management device. It is simply one amongst a number of ways of identifying potentially fruitful paths and of becoming conscious of cul-de-sacs.

A SWOT analysis attempts to set out the internal strengths and weaknesses of an organization, alongside the external opportunities and threats that it faces. A particular strength of an organization is set alongside a corresponding weakness and these are both matched to relevant external opportunities and threats. The aim of such an analysis is not to create some sort of 'balance' (a particular temptation for Anglican churches). Rather the aim is to create better self-knowledge, whether for church leaders, for church areas or for local congregations.

For example, a particular university might have a very strong track record of research and teaching in the humanities but a rather weak record in the natural sciences. If leaders of that university are wise, they will look to opportunities for research and student recruitment in this area of strength. They will probably regard a government policy favouring the natural sciences at the expense of the humanities as a threat. However, if they are unwise they will, without providing any additional resources, market the natural sciences of that university as its strongest feature in the hope that the outside world will not notice.

Quite simply, a SWOT analysis allows any leader and any member of an organization to be frank about its own strengths and weaknesses in order to determine its objectives in the outside world upon which it ultimately depends. A SWOT analysis might persuade leaders of an organization to change direction dramatically. That, however, is usually a long-term objective. In the short-term a SWOT analysis should help leaders and members to discern the realizable opportunities of their organization.

Of course SWOT analysis is not the only way of doing this. Another way, for instance, of achieving the same result is to analyse everything in terms of a series of objectives. There are long-term objectives, middle-term objectives and immediate objectives. There are attainable objectives and there are unattainable objectives. There are key objectives which are central to an institution's mission statement, there are peripheral objectives, and there are spurious objectives which are at odds with the mission statement. Nevertheless a SWOT analysis does have the merit of being both clear and familiar within many universities, businesses and, increasingly, churches too.

In the following chart we offer a very summary SWOT analysis of the Church of England today. Naturally others may well consider different features of the Church of England to be more important. This is intended simply as an illustration of our perception of our own Church today. Such an analysis is something that all denominations could do for themselves – as could individual dioceses and parishes. At all of these different levels, a SWOT analysis can be a useful aid for strategic church leadership.

SWOT analysis – Church of England			
Strengths	*Weaknesses*	*Opportunities*	*Threats*
Parochial	Declining	Ubiquity	Marginalism
Inclusive	Amorphous	Toleration	Secularism
Indigenous	Myopic	Establishment	Apathy
Well-resourced	Subsidized	Mission	Lethargy

The first set of features is concerned with the physical presence of the Church of England as a parochial rather than a gathered church. Both of us have experience of gathered churches and are aware that they too have strengths. However we believe that in many areas of England the parochial nature of the Church of England (and in Scotland of the Church of Scotland) is one of its enduring assets. In many rural and suburban areas the parish church remains a focus of religious and often secular life. It is not simply the minority of people who regularly go to church in a Church of England building. Rather it is the broad population of many rural and suburban

areas who still regard the parish church as 'their' church –
whether for rites of passage, for school celebrations, for civic
occasions, or simply for its presence in their midst. Taken
together this spectrum of possibilities offers leaders in the
Church of England a remarkable degree of local contact with
the population at large. Most political parties would love to be
so well endowed.

Of course there are also weaknesses in this parochial contact.
Most obviously it is declining. We have already spelt out this
point in earlier chapters. The most recent attendance figures
for the Church of England are hardly encouraging. A very
sharp leader in the *Church Times*, noting a rise in general giving
but a decline of 3 per cent attendance in a single year, argued
as follows:

> A few years ago, the release of attendance figures for the
> Church of England was accompanied by some combination
> of the words 'smaller', 'leaner' and 'more committed'.
> Churchgoing is down, we were told, but giving is up. It
> sounded as if the Church were shedding its unwanted fat –
> nominal, unproductive Christians – but keeping its core. It
> was nothing of the sort. If one considered the statistics with
> clear-sighted observation, the downward trend was caused
> by older, poorer churchgoers dying off, as they do, and not
> being replaced fast enough by younger ones. Nowadays, the
> talk is more commonly of 'gentle slides'. The misplaced
> buoyancy has been replaced by mild depression. Meanwhile
> the trend has not altered. New people are coming to church,
> but not in sufficient numbers to counteract those who fall
> away . . . The sacrifice that the increased giving represents
> deserves to be commended. But a Church whose regular
> attendance is likely to drop below one million within four
> or five years has little to congratulate itself upon. (22 July
> 1995)

It is not just that this decline produces a generalized air of
depression which, in turn, makes regular churchgoing in the
Church of England ever less attractive. That in itself is serious
enough. Rather it is that, in some areas of the country,
Anglican churchgoing is now so low that the parochial nature
of churches there has all but disappeared. In many inner urban
and urban priority areas this is already the case. The fear is that

this may increasingly happen in rural and suburban areas as well.

Does this matter to the Church of England? We believe that it does. The parochial system has offered a unique spectrum of opportunities in England. Its demise could signal increasing marginalization. Certainly the Turnbull Report is convinced that 'the parochial system provides the theologically significant building blocks of the Church of England's strategy for service. The gospel of redeeming love and sacrifice must take root in the immediate neighbourhood' (para. 2.11). It is easy to idealize this parochial system. Historically it may at times have supported feudal and authoritarian patterns of local ministry. However, where it exists in parts of both the Church of England and the Church of Scotland today, it can still offer local churches genuine opportunities.

First the opportunities. Sheer ubiquity is the most obvious opportunity in society at large that has followed from the parochial system of the Church of England. At local level, parish priests have often been intimately connected with the civic and cultural life of their parishes. At national level, the archbishops and senior diocesan bishops have had a unique role in the House of Lords and in the national media. Many American colleagues, despite coming from an environment of much higher regular churchgoing, are astonished at the regular coverage given in the media especially to the Archbishop of Canterbury.

Next the threats. Ubiquity goes hand in hand with the threat of marginalization. As attendances decline, and are seen to decline, so the Church of England is increasingly regarded in society at large as a marginal institution. For the last two decades a declining number of people have been offering themselves for candidacy for ordination. Clergy often voice the opinion that they are regarded as largely marginal figures by members of other professions. And senior clergy, too, often feel themselves to be increasingly marginalized in a pluralistic, let alone 'secular', society. A series of newspaper exposures, giving the impression that it is their private lives not their religious views which are of interest, has reinforced this feeling.

If this part of the SWOT analysis is in any way accurate, it does seem to offer some clues to current leaders in the Church of England. The parochial system offers real opportunities in many areas. Suppose for a moment that stemming or even reversing churchgoing decline became a central objective of Anglican bishops. If they really succeeded in this objective, fewer opportunities may be lost in the future. Even the threat of marginalization may be linked to a public perception of general decline in churchgoing. Any institution that is seen to be in a state of irreversible decline is likely to be marginalized. Physical presence is not everything, but it is nevertheless important.

The next set of features in our SWOT analysis of the Church of England concern its culture. Ever since its beginning as a separate denomination, the Church of England has been characterized by its inclusiveness. The Book of Common Prayer was deliberately framed to be inclusive. For example, those with competing eucharistic theologies – high and low church alike – could find echoes of their various positions in its service of Holy Communion. The Alternative Service Book is even more inclusive, offering four distinct eucharistic prayers and hundreds of small variations, alongside a more traditional liturgy. Its successor in 2000 may offer greater variety still. Choice abounds. Some theologians have depicted this as the Church of England's 'comprehensiveness', others find the term too woolly. Our own preference is for the term 'inclusive'. Unlike exclusive churches, such as the Roman Catholic Church in its traditional form, or exclusive sects, such as the Exclusive Brethren, the Church of England has for long been tolerant of theological differences and of individuals who use its offices only occasionally.

This inclusiveness has ensured that religious toleration (with occasional lapses) has for long been an important part of English culture. Unlike many parts of Roman Catholic Europe, anticlericalism has not been a striking feature of English culture. An inclusive Church has seldom polarized the population. Other than through baptism (often soon after birth) the Church of England has not even had a coherent concept of church membership. Occasional and regular churchgoers could both feel that they were genuinely part of the same Church.

Not surprisingly there are weaknesses and threats associated with this position. A persistent criticism of the Church of England, especially from those belonging to more exclusive churches, is that it is amorphous. And the recurrent fear is that its inclusiveness does little to stem, and may even encourage, growing secularism – that is, secularism understood as the gradual abandonment of all religious beliefs and practices. If amorphousness is the internal weakness, secularism is the outside threat.

There is nothing inevitable about this internal weakness and outside threat. A past generation of sociologists often concluded that secularism was an ineluctable process gradually sweeping all things religious before it. It is more common today to hear sociologists talk about pluralism and religious variability. Resurgent forms of religious fundamentalism, increasing religious pluralism and experimentation, as well as sharp secularism, all seem to co-exist in the same societies. In this situation there surely is still a place for an inclusive Church, albeit for a Church which is fully aware of the dangers of becoming too amorphous. Anglican leaders should rightly keep inclusivity as an objective.

This point links to the next set of features, which are all concerned with the place of the Church of England specifically within English society. Its strength is that it is a genuinely indigenous Church. It arose from the peculiarities of Tudor politics and it has retained, through its established position, a constitutional role within English society. This has always provided its leaders with unique access to those in power. Itself largely lacking formal power (unlike the Vatican), its leaders none the less have often been extremely close to those in power. This has sometimes given them unique opportunities of quiet influence.

The weakness of such an indigenous Church is that it risks, quite literally, becoming too provincial. Even within the Anglican Communion the Church of England has sometimes been regarded as too myopic. Notably during the controversy over the ordination of women, some parts of the Anglican Communion felt exasperated that the issue was too often debated within the Church of England as if it had not already been discussed and decided elsewhere in the Communion. For example, relations with the Roman Catholic Church were discussed as if it were the Church of England's ordination practices alone which mattered.

If myopia is the internal weakness in this area, then apathy is the external threat. It cannot be claimed that the establishment or non-establishment of the Church of England is an issue of national concern. Occasionally a politician will raise the prospect of disestablishment. Yet it is difficult to imagine that any modern government would be prepared to give the Church of England the necessary parliamentary time to effect it, even if the General Synod were strongly pressing for it. In Wales and Ireland, in a very different era, the issue of disestablishment did become sufficiently important politically for the government to act. In the modern era it is surely inconceivable. It is now an issue greeted with considerable public apathy.

The final set of features returns to the issue of resources and finance which have already been outlined in earlier chapters and to which we will return later. Despite its enormous losses, the Church Commissioners are still responsible for assets of well over two billion pounds. As the Turnbull Report recognizes, the Church of England thus remains a well-resourced Church with many opportunities for using these resources for effective mission. Unfortunately it has all too often squandered these resources in the past. Subsidy, we argued earlier, has been one of the Church of England's most persistent weaknesses. The external threat associated with its subsidized inefficiency has been lethargy. Instead of local congregations being challenged to be self-supporting, a heavily subsidized ministry and buildings has been supplied from central resources, whether the latter are used for communal worship or not. By now our argument should be very familiar.

SWOT analysis is simply a technique. What is important is that strategic leaders learn to discriminate. Particularly, that they learn to identify strengths and match them to opportunities when determining objectives. Conversely, they should be frank about weaknesses and well aware of threats. No institution, let alone a church, will be without weaknesses and threats. It is crucial that church leaders become sensitive to them and incorporate a knowledge of them sensitively into a strategic plan. But that is for the next chapter.

CHAPTER SIX
Strategic Planning

When Silas and Timothy came from Macedonia, Paul devoted himself exclusively to preaching, testifying to the people that Jesus was the Christ. But when they opposed Paul and became abusive, he shook out his clothes in protest and said to them, 'Your blood be on your heads! I am clear of my responsibility. From now on I will go to the Gentiles.' Then Paul left the synagogue and went next door to the house of Titius Justus, a worshipper of God. Crispus, the synagogue ruler, and his entire household believed in the Lord; and many of the Corinthians who heard him believed and were baptized. (Acts 18.5–8)

STRATEGIC PLANNING IN THE UNIVERSITIES

Over the last ten years, the universities have learned, painfully and rather slowly, how to respond strategically to change. And in so doing they have changed themselves – becoming more flexible and forward looking.

What is it that the universities have learned that may be of value to the churches? Foremost, that motivation is all – people must believe that their institution has a future and that, through their work, they can affect that future. The role of a strategic leader is to release energies, to enable people to develop a feeling of worth in their job, and especially to release their energies in a way that makes sense for the institution as a whole. This means there must be common and shared priorities; clear and overriding objectives and agreed methods for reaching and testing those objectives. In short, new-style university leaders need to have a strategic plan.

At the University of East Anglia, Derek Burke encouraged people to ask 'What sort of University do we want to be in the year 2000?' Then, the second step: 'How are we going to get from where we are now to where we want to be?' These two processes – identifying the main objectives and the major strategies to achieve them – are the key initial elements of a strategic plan. Business has valuable experience to draw from in this process.

Identifying the main objectives is not as easy as it sounds, mainly because everyone thinks they know what these objectives are, even though they may actually never have been discussed. And when they are discussed there is often disagreement. It is too easy to finish any discussion by saying 'we don't want to change at all' or 'we want to change but only after reaching unanimous agreement', or 'we want to change but . . .' Then follows a series of conditions, such as 'we want to keep all current staff in employment'.

Another problem is that institutions – businesses, universities and churches – accumulate all sorts of additional tasks. These may be worthy, and indeed have their defenders, but are they all necessary? A fruitful way the University of East Anglia found to see a way through this was to start again, and to ask 'What do we *have* to do to stay in business?' 'Business' here means not just staying solvent, although that is necessary, but rather retaining a sense of identity and purpose for the institution, so that everyone can see what it is for. In other words there needs to be a shared vision emerging from analysis and debate. Universities are good at analysis and debate – like churches – and much better at these than at decision making – again like churches. Debate, of course, means disagreement, yet different views, courteously put, can be very constructive in drawing out the real issues. However, anger can be deeply destructive and one of the tasks of strategic leadership is to encourage debate while controlling anger.

The main objectives – and there should be no more than five of them – should be concise, realistic and *testable*. That is, in five year's time it should be possible to determine whether the objectives, broken down year by year, have been reached or not. Bland statements are of no use at all to an institution. One useful test of an objective is to know what it excludes and what priorities it implies. Agreed objectives can then lead to agreed strategies. How are we going to get from where we are now to where we want to be? The setting of priorities means that some objectives are more important than others. To put this into practice, the resource allocation must be selective, so that high priority areas get more than low priority areas. Or to put it the other way round, it is only if the resource allocation can be done selectively that the priorities are of any use.

Selectivity has to work both ways; money has to be given to high priority areas *and* withdrawn from low priority areas. Sometimes withdrawing money is comparatively easy – a project coming to a natural end, someone retiring – but more often than not, withdrawal of funds means terminating good, but not essential, projects and the people involved either being transferred to other positions or losing their jobs. Then comes the real test of leadership and commitment – can the leader bring it about and will the institution, church or university, accept it as regrettable but fair?

Sometimes the savings cannot be made immediately, but are possible over two to three years, although that means running a deficit. Beware – such proposals have a habit of slipping, so that these two to three years become five to six years and then ultimately nothing happens. Strategic leaders need steely resolve not to be deflected.

Every organization has some things which do not have to be continued – they have been preserved because of sentiment, political sensitivities or, most commonly, because no one wants to take a clear decision and, above all, because leaders want to be liked by everyone. Perhaps once that was possible when there was new money available every year in the universities. Today there is not and all that a university leader can hope for is respect. Being liked by all is impossible, and that is not something that Christian leaders today typically like or expect. Yet the quotation at the beginning of this chapter paints a very different picture of church leadership. Paul in Acts was thoroughly prepared to face antagonism once he was clear about his priorities. Ultimately the choice is often between the survival of the institution and one's personal popularity. There is no real choice when it is put like that. Sometimes a strategic leader needs to act decisively on behalf of future generations.

Since withdrawing money from an institution usually means losing jobs, people do sometimes have to be persuaded to leave. And that is not easy. People have, of course, legal rights, and they may have personal commitments that make losing their job traumatic for all, but such issues do have to be faced. Retraining for another position is sometimes a possibility – but again experience shows that those who are retrainable have usually seen what is coming and have already made a move. Those that are left must be treated with dignity and courtesy – nobody should be humiliated – yet action must still be firm.

Telling someone face-to-face that they need to leave can be very painful, but on occasions it will need to be done, and done properly. Leaders of an institution must give a lead here: it is unfair to leave it to more junior staff. Strategic leadership must come from the front, so it is necessary to explain courteously, but firmly, that the institution can no longer afford some members of staff, and that since their particular task is complete – or is to be passed to another – they must leave. In leaving, the institution will be supportive and generous. On the other hand, if they stay, they will find themselves increasingly isolated from their colleagues, without value to the institution, and in the end totally dispirited – conflict and hostility are inevitable.

All companies have been through this, though some have handled it better than others. All universities have been through this too. There was one department at the University of East Anglia that had to lose 33 per cent of its budget, another half its staff, and another 75 per cent of its staff, all over three to four years. Why, asks Derek Burke, should the churches not be able to face the same issues? Is there anything sacrosanct about working for churches? Fewer and fewer laypeople today think so.

But restructuring must be a prelude to rebuilding. People must know that there is a future which is worth working for. It is important to start investing as soon as possible. Universities have found top slicing a good way to do this – taking say 3 to 5 per cent out of everyone's budget, and then making it available for new projects for anywhere in the institution – *as long as they fit with the agreed strategy*. Then there is something to work for.

So resource allocation must be:

- absolutely in line with agreed priorities;

- as fair as possible;

- open and accountable: there must be no secret pockets.

And the golden rule – a budget is a budget is a budget. No budget holder must be allowed to overspend – and if they do, and some always do, they must carry the deficit into the next year.

Tensions of course abound – in universities the sciences think the humanities are over-funded and vice-versa, and everyone thinks the central administration is over-funded. And they sometimes are. It is quite difficult for administrators to be as tough with their own budget as with those of others. Strategic leaders must not have favourites.

But along with central resource allocation there must be delegated financial decision making. Universities increasingly find, as many others have, that those closest to decisions make the best decisions. To enable this to happen more effectively, most universities now run on a series of budget centres – Chemistry, Law, Administration, the Library and so forth – each with its own finances which it must balance.

An important assumption behind this process is a break away from incremental budgeting and towards zero-based budgeting. Under incremental budgeting historical patterns largely dictate the way resources are allocated in the present. As long as they can still be afforded, jobs and structures are funded because they have been so funded in the past. Historic costs are carried over without question into the future. However, when finances become more constrained, incremental budgeting dictates that cuts are spread evenly over all sectors. In the middle 1980s the University Grants Committee broke away from incremental budgeting and replaced it with a formula driven process. According to this, all universities received the same amount of money to teach students in, say, chemistry wherever they were in Britain and regardless of what individual universities were spending. This process of zero-based budgeting forced the universities radically to reassess all of their expenditure and was an essential basis for their expansion in the early 1990s.

Underlying all of this must be a *realistic* estimate of income for, say, five to ten years ahead. All institutions tend to be optimistic, so the estimate must assume a pessimistic projection of income from investment, gifts and so forth. What it must *not* do is assume, without any basis, that there will be enough income to meet both current expenditure and all the new things that people would like to do. The result of the latter is a wish-list rather than a budget.

It is important, too, to distinguish between non-recurrent expenditure – for example, for buildings and repairs – and recurrent expenditure, especially salaries. The churches, like the universities, spend a very high proportion of their income on salaries – an expenditure which runs on and grows from year to year. Eventually this can consume the whole of an institution's budget. Then there will be lots of people, but nothing for them to work with – not even any money for paper clips!

STRATEGIC PLANNING IN THE CHURCHES

Is such a model of strategic planning appropriate for churches? There are many who are likely to be highly sceptical at this point in our argument. There may seem something rather too ruthless about this style of planning for churches. Colleagues and friends sometimes argue that churches must not replicate the faults of the current management culture. Chronic job insecurity, obsession with budgets, oversimplistic single-mindedness, undervaluing of supposedly 'unproductive' colleagues, viewing people solely in terms of their market worth, and reducing everything to measurable outcomes, are only some of the faults that are seen in this management culture. It is not the business of churches, so they argue, to surrender to this alien culture. Churches should continue to witness to the virtues of consensus, harmony, non-measurable qualities, and full employment.

Ironically the latter are not the virtues of church leadership that we have noticed in the Acts of the Apostles. The quotation at the head of this chapter paints a very different picture: 'when they opposed Paul and became abusive, he shook out his clothes in protest and said to them, "Your blood be on your heads!"' (18.6) These are not the words of consensus, harmony or conciliation. There are, of course, some moments in Acts when there are attempts to limit conflict and to reach agreement corporately. Most obviously this happens in chapter 15. But even this starts with the observation that Paul and Barnabas were in 'sharp dispute and debate' with other Christians about the necessity of circumcision (15.2). Further, as we noted earlier, the same chapter concludes with Paul and Barnabas themselves having 'such a sharp disagreement that they parted company' (15.39). Throughout Acts Paul, especially, is depicted as a church leader whose strong vision and sense of mission brought him into conflict both with his fellow Christians and with his fellow Jews. Repeatedly he saw a clear task before him and was not prepared to let either his friends or his adversaries deflect him from this task.

Once again it is important not to be misunderstood at this point. We are not, of course, claiming that a conflictual style of leadership, which deliberately courts discord, is desirable in the churches. Local congregations typically consist of (predominantly female) unpaid volunteers with a single (usually male) paid member. In this respect they differ even from universities. Churches are certainly not aggressive, commercial businesses. The livelihood of very few church members depends upon the 'success' or 'failure' of churches. In addition, some of the most important Christian virtues are indeed elusive – even the terms 'success' and 'failure' must be put firmly in quotation marks every time they are used about churches. Neither of us wishes to 'reduce' churches solely to budgets and to measurable outcomes. All of this we regard with horror.

Rather our claim is that church leaders do already have implicit styles of leadership and that, compared with many other similar organizations, these implicit styles are now widely regarded as outmoded. Consensus management and incremental budgeting are still prevalent in churches at a time when they are largely discredited elsewhere. Church leaders often look like rather old-fashioned managers – despite the fact that they often deny that they are 'managers' at all. They tend to be so committed to a consensus style of leadership, as well as to an incremental style of budgeting, that they imagine that these styles are somehow more inherently Christian than modern styles of leadership based upon strategic planning. We believe, in contrast, that none of these styles of leadership and planning are inherently Christian or unchristian. The way they are used can indeed be more or less Christian. However in themselves they are rather styles which are simply more or less efficient.

Some of the faults resulting from a thoughtless or ruthless use of strategic planning have already been noted. What is sometimes not observed is that both a consensus style of leadership and an incremental style of budgeting can also be morally flawed. Once it is known by obstinate minorities that their leaders will not proceed with policies unless there is the full agreement of all the people concerned, they soon become conscious that they have in fact been given a powerful veto. The few soon learn that they can hold back the many – whether for valid reasons or merely out of personal prejudice. Precisely this has been one of the most difficult obstacles of church reform in the twentieth century. In hierarchical, non-democratic churches, such as the Roman Catholic Church, liturgical reforms, for example, have typically been achieved by *fiat*. In the Church of England, in contrast, it took well over half a century to effect significant liturgical reforms – which are still rejected by a traditionalist minority. On a variety of key issues organized minorities in the Church of England have been able to block change – sometimes for decades.

Most seriously of all, consensus leadership has tended to stunt the missionary role of the Church of England. Those clergy who have no interest in mission, and who regard the numbers of people coming to public worship as irrelevant, have an equal say with those who do believe in mission and are deeply concerned about numbers. Pastoral committees in dioceses are likely to contain representatives of both groups. And, precisely because the leaders of such committees are usually so committed to consensus, they often fail to adopt strategic plans or to implement them rigorously, let alone test them, if they do adopt them.

Consensus assumptions are often built into the very com-position of a typical pastoral committee. Competing groups and interests are represented to give a 'balanced' membership. For years Robin Gill was puzzled by the mission inactivity of one pastoral committee until he examined its composition more carefully. What he discovered was that leaders of the committee deliberately sought to balance rural and urban cler-gy in a diocese whose population remained overwhelmingly urban. This ensured that when parish vacancies occurred a disproportionate amount of clergy were deployed into rural areas, their salaries in effect being subsidized by wealthier urban parishes. The clergy on the committee from urban areas, in turn, seldom challenged this system of rural deployment and subsidy since they were unable to match the rural clergy's knowledge of the parishes in which vacancies occurred.

A very similar point is made in the Turnbull Report. In one of its most hard hitting paragraphs it maintains:

The Church's management of its human resources – its most precious resource – is characterised by an incoherence in policy aggravated by confused structures. In relation to the ordained ministry, for example, there is no single plan for the optimum numbers needed and how they are to be trained and deployed, and for making the necessary financial projections and plans for how the costs of their stipends and pensions are to be met. Ideally, the Church should have a strategy which is mission-led rather than resource-led. It should look at how many clergy it needs to meet its aspirations in serving the nation as a whole. It cannot, however, ignore the question of how to secure the resources to support them. The Church should also, for example, ensure that its discussions about the nature of the Church's current mission are taken into account when candidates are selected for ordination . . . Central and diocesan bodies often strive to do their best, sometimes taking on responsibilities which are not within their core functions, but gaps remain. There is no strategic overview. (para. 3.10)

Surely it is inconceivable that any secular organization could be run on such a basis. It is imperative that church leaders listen carefully to these strictures from the Turnbull Report.

In addition to consensus, a second assumption lying behind this example is again the use of incremental budgeting. In chapter 3 incremental budgeting was seen as the system of resource allocation in which allowances for inflation had been added year by year without any questions being asked about whether the final distribution actually made sense. Like consensus leadership, incremental budgeting seeks to be fair. Just as consensus leadership seeks to give an equal voice to majorities and minorities alike, so incremental budgeting seeks to give equal (even if diminishing) financial resources to all. Unfortunately, both are strategies for inaction: both are deeply conservative. They often ensure that an organization is unable to change and must accept, instead, its own gradual demise.

Incremental budgeting within churches does little to help them respond effectively to rapid changes in society. It has ensured that the Church of England and, to a lesser extent, the Methodist Church, has remained disproportionately rural long after most of the population moved to urban and suburban

areas. In both denominations rural church buildings still out-
number their urban and suburban counterparts. And both (but
especially the Church of England) continue to subsidize rural
clerical salaries. The Church of England has also continued to
maintain many city-centre parishes (the City churches in
London are an obvious and long-standing example), which
have long since lost effective surrounding populations. Incremental budgeting, allowing an unquestioned use of subsidy, is
largely responsible for this.

In contrast, strategic planning would suggest that jobs and
the budgets that support them always have to be justified – even
when these budgets are apparently still in surplus. This is the
essence of zero-based budgeting. Strategic planning builds a
system of rigorous inspection into the process of deployment at
every level. An appointment resulting from a vacancy has to be
justified in terms of the aims of the organization as a whole. It
is not sufficient to argue that that particular post has always
been filled in the past. It must still be needed and it should
preferably have potential to be developed further in the future.
Otherwise the resources might be deployed more effectively in
some other area of the organization.

It is time to return to our mission statement for the churches
today:

*The central aim of churches in modern Britain is the communal worship of
God in Christ through the Spirit, teaching and moulding as many lives and
structures as deeply as possible through this worship.*

If this became the basis for strategic planning in the churches,
they really could be transformed.

Strategic planning would treat the fostering of communal
worship of God in Christ through the Spirit as the chief
priority of churches. The extent to which churches lead more
rather than fewer people to take part in such worship could
clearly be monitored. Naturally it would be important to keep
a careful qualitative check on this worship and particularly on
the (sometimes fairly elusive) ways in which worship might
teach and mould both individual lives and structures. After
the sad events that surrounded the bold liturgical experiment,
the Nine O'clock Service, at Sheffield, this point hardly
needs to be stressed. Checks on outcomes – the theme of
chapter 8 – are an essential part of a strategic process.

Accountability is both a theological and an ethical require-
ment.

Given this priority for worship, those churches and congregations which share and foster it would be given preference to
those which do not. The pattern of this worship will need
to respond to local needs and will differ from place to place.
The test is how effective it actually is in promoting Christian
worship in that particular place. Naturally this implies that
resources would be deliberately shifted around churches in the
light of this priority. Some church buildings will need to be
closed and new congregations will have to be started. The
latter may or may not imply church buildings. There is
growing evidence that congregation 'planting' can be achieved
within existing church buildings in the form of new parallel
services. School buildings too can be used. Interestingly some
schools have recently become rather keener than a decade ago
to earn additional revenue in this way. A policy of top-slicing
would suggest that a central planning group in every denomination should seek to identify genuine opportunities for growth
in communal worship; should strategically use a proportion of
the funds from all of the churches to pump-prime this growth;
and should then carefully monitor whether or not qualitative
and quantitative growth has actually been achieved.

Doubtless there will be many failures in such a strategic planning policy as well as considerable criticism, even conflict.
Church leaders embarking on such a programme must expect
both. The central message in this chapter is that they should
not allow either initial failure or internal criticism to deflect
them from their task. It is difficult to achieve growth in any
organization without some failures. As will be seen later, initial
failure is less of a problem than an inability to know when
objectives have actually been achieved. Some failures are to be
expected; likewise criticism. Effective church leaders must
expect both. As we pointed out earlier, wishing to be loved by
everyone should not be their priority. We fear that all too often
it is.

CHAPTER SEVEN
Strategic Ownership

At this point Festus interrupted Paul's defence (before King Agrippa). 'You are out of your mind, Paul!' he shouted. 'Your great learning is driving you insane.'

'I am not insane, most excellent Festus,' Paul replied. 'What I am saying is true and reasonable. The king is familiar with these things, and I can speak freely to him. I am convinced that none of this has escaped his notice, because it was not done in a corner. King Agrippa, do you believe the prophets? I know you do.'

Then Agrippa said to Paul, 'Do you think that in such a short time you can persuade me to be a Christian?' (Acts 26.24–28)

Ownership is crucial to strategic leadership. It can also be its most difficult feature. In the Acts of the Apostles not even Paul's best attempts to share his vision with King Agrippa were successful. Time and again Paul is pictured attempting to convince uncomprehending, and sometimes belligerent authorities and yet failing. Effective leaders have a vision, have a clear notion of priorities and objectives, and then they attempt to share this vision with others, to enable others to own it too. Once a vision is thoroughly owned by members of any group or institution, then creative change is possible. But the path to ownership is not always easy, especially in institutions such as universities and churches. Whereas a business might be able to sack employees who do not share its vision, the autonomy of lecturers and clergy largely protects them from such measures. Instead they must be persuaded. Strategic leaders in universities and churches are likely to have a hard struggle to get others to share and own their vision.

OWNERSHIP IN THE UNIVERSITIES

The change in leadership style in universities over the last ten years or so has largely been driven by falling income, making it impossible for them to continue everything that was previously done. Choosing rationally what ought still to be done and what should be dropped is what strategic planning is about. Persuading other people to accept this process is what strategic ownership is about.

We have already noted that, in the 1960s, with increasing funds available annually, universities used to work by 'incremental budgeting'. They simply added the same percentage increase to every historic item of expenditure. There was a general four or five per cent increase, certainly enough to cover inflation, and each university then argued about the rest. Some of the argument took place within departments, some within faculty and some at senate. In the last of these, sixty to one hundred people, with the vice-chancellor in the chair, argued until nearly everyone agreed. Admittedly the senate worked from a series of recommendations of a small committee. Nevertheless, it would reject or alter these recommendations without hesitation – after all, it was the supreme academic body. The vice-chancellor was often little more than a neutral chair.

Most universities abandoned that process in the 1980s. Falling income, distrust of incremental budgeting, but above all, a clear realization that this process was going nowhere, led to its demise. There was a more effective way; and the recommendations of the Jarratt Report in 1985 started a process that has continued for over a decade, that of strategic budgeting. But how was the change to the new style to be brought about?

First, there had to be a general acceptance that the old way was obsolete. Incremental budgeting and consensus decision making will only work when there is more money coming into institutions every year; it cannot deal with declining budgets. No large group can decide where and what to cut back. But it took time for this to be generally realized in the universities – time spent searching for any conceivable way of keeping the old system going. Using up the reserves, going into deficit, daring the Government to let a university go bankrupt – all were proposed. It was the leadership's role to explain patiently, but firmly, why none of these would work. Patience was essential; people's concerns about their own future did have to be taken seriously, but they could not be allowed to rule the institution's future.

Finding a new way certainly was not easy at the University of East Anglia. Staff felt threatened, undervalued and angry – angry both with Government and with the university leadership. It took months until staff accepted that, although they still thought their treatment unfair, the financial problems would not go away. A solution had to be found, but where and how? The second stage was debate about the best route ahead. Debate was focused by asking each department and cost centre to carry out its own SWOT analysis and to draw up a series of prioritized objectives. The initial attempts were not very helpful. One department had thirteen objectives, all equally important, and another had no weaknesses. But discussion with the senior leadership, criticism from peers in other departments and, ultimately, their own academic honesty led to more realistic analysis – and academics are good at analysis – and to feasible objectives. The third stage was to match the SWOT analysis and objectives to the new, lower resource level. That was hard because it meant job losses. Again and again, proposals had to be referred back for reworking, since it was essential that the final proposals met the twin demands of strategy and budget. It took months. Often several alternative strategies were explored in parallel before a choice was made, and frequently the initial strategy was improved by debate, albeit slowly and in stages. The final outcome was in every case better than the initial objectives from the department and, importantly, better than those proposed initially by the leadership.

This process can be described by the phrase 'top-down, bottom-up, top-down'. The top must initiate. It is the task of strategic leadership to set the challenge, to refuse to let the institution fudge the issue, to ensure that the real questions are dealt with and, over and over again, to bring the debate back to central issues. Then all those deeply involved must respond: question, argue, propose alternatives 'bottom-up'. Finally, the leadership must take the best proposals through for final approval. These proposals might not be universally agreed. Consensus is not always possible, but there comes a point when nearly everyone realizes that the current proposals are the best that can be obtained, and then leaders must act. Strategic leaders must, of course, take the criticism and perhaps even the opprobrium for the final decisions – after all, that is what they are paid to do – to lead. There has to be a desk where 'the buck stops'.

Crucially, this process establishes strategic ownership by as many people as possible. That is, the process of debate has ensured that all those involved have been able to criticize and propose, and that most of them have accepted that the final objectives are the best available. When most people own objectives, final approval is greatly simplified and there is a good chance that the eventual decisions will be put into practice.

Strategic ownership is different from consultation. Strategic ownership means joint discussion about objectives that are to be implemented and jointly monitored. Consultation, on the other hand, seeks people's views, but makes no commitment about the final outcome. Strategic ownership accepts that all parties are involved in finding, agreeing upon and testing a solution. It is, of course, much harder work for leaders than, say, acting as a neutral chair in a debate that is trying to find consensus, or alternatively, making executive decisions after a period of consultation. Yet a strategic plan without ownership is a waste of time; in a university, or a church, it will be no more than a paper plan.

Some will argue that promoting and carrying through such a process dangerously weakens leadership. That is not so, but it is not an easy style of leadership. At the start it means making proposals that invite criticism and that will inevitably be changed. It also involves patient hours of discussion, listening to criticism, but refusing to let people avoid dealing with the issues. It involves getting approval for objectives which will not please everyone and it means taking the responsibility for seeing that the plan is implemented and monitored.

Strategic leaders need to be resolute, as always, but they also need to be flexible – and they need constantly to challenge their institution. For by the time the plan has been debated, agreed and implementation commenced, the world will have changed again and new initiatives are needed. Strategic leaders need continually to initiate and innovate, putting out proposals that may not readily be accepted but which are essential if the institution is not to stagnate. A changing world calls for a new style of leadership – but one interestingly that is rather closer to that of Acts than is the consensus style of leadership which still predominates in British churches. The strategic leader must be driven by a vision – a vision of the role that the institution can play in a changing world – and by a desire to share this vision with others. For, unless visions are shared and widely owned, institutions tend to perish.

OWNERSHIP IN THE CHURCHES

Church leaders, too, need to move away from an incremental and consensus style of leadership. A more strategic understanding of both budgets and decision making is imperative. The previous chapter set out our criticisms of incremental forms of budgeting and consensus approaches to decision making. It is time now to spell out the positive implications of this part of our analysis of strategic church leadership.

First, there are budgets. Given the long-term decline in British churchgoing and the recent investment losses of the Church Commissioners, it is only too easy to spend the whole time considering church finances. This is an obvious danger. Nevertheless it is crucial that churches do have an effective form of budgeting. Without it clergy cannot be paid, pensions cannot be provided, church buildings cannot be maintained, and even church leadership cannot be financially supported.

Instructively, budgeting is the source of one of the earliest church disputes in Acts. The author recounts (possibly a little idealistically):

> All the believers were one in heart and mind. No-one claimed that any of his possessions was his own, but they shared everything they had . . . There was no needy persons among them. For from time to time those who owned lands or houses sold them, brought the money from the sales and put it at the apostles' feet, and it was distributed to anyone as he had need. (4.32–35)

However, Ananias and Sapphira have held back. Peter is exasperated:

> Ananias, how is it that Satan has so filled your heart that you have lied to the Holy Spirit and have kept for yourself some of the money you received for the land? Didn't it belong to you before it was sold? And after it was sold,

wasn't the money at your disposal? What made you think of doing such a thing? You have not lied to men but to God. (5.3–4)

At the heart of this dispute is the issue of truthfulness. The couple are exposed as hypocrites before God. However, in addition, there are two quite different concepts of budgeting involved in the dispute. The one practised by the apostles and, ostensibly, by Ananias and Sapphira, is based on total giving and holding money in common. The other, secretly practised by Ananias and Sapphira, holds back a proportion from the common pool. A fatal mixture of hypocrisy and disputed finances.

How do churches today avoid such a mixture? All of the ingredients are still present. Local church councils and vestries often express anger with church authorities. 'Church leaders just want our money, they don't want to take notice of our views.' 'Why should we give to central church funds when they cannot even look after our investments properly?' As church-going continues to decline, and as clergy pensions, let alone salaries, become increasingly difficult to finance, such local reactions are likely to become sharper still.

A greater sense of ownership and accountability are essential if congregations are to flourish. And for this to happen, local budget holding is a key feature. It is at this point that our proposals go considerably beyond the Turnbull Report. The need for tighter financial control and strategic planning in the Church of England at a national level is clearly recognized by the Turnbull Report. It argues for a National Council which will have considerable powers in this direction. Commendably both of these functions – financial control and strategic planning – are remits of this National Council. In effective organizations they are inextricably linked. However, in seeking to raise money for dioceses, and particularly for poorer dioceses, the Report makes no mention of a role for this National Council in promoting, let alone auditing, local ownership. We will return to the question of local audit and accountability in the next chapter. Here our concern is with genuinely local ownership in the form of self-funding churches.

There is extensive research showing that self-funding churches are much more likely to flourish and grow than subsidized churches. Subsidized churches have a tendency to lack motivation to change, to lose any impetus towards evangelism, and to show signs of dependency. In contrast, self-funding churches have to change if they are to survive, tend to be much keener on evangelism, and often show signs of independence. Precisely because of this spirit of independence, they may appear troublesome to some church leaders. They may be more likely than other churches to challenge central church policies and to question the use made of their contributions to central funds. In addition, they may well wish to have more say over their own clergy appointments and expect their clergy, once appointed, to live up to their own ideals. A wise church leadership should look at all of these tendencies of self-funding churches as opportunities rather than as threats. Without such features it is difficult to see how churches as a whole might once again grow.

Local budget holding gives congregations, or clusters of congregations, an important measure of ownership. Once members of a congregation know that it is their resources alone which will pay for their ordained ministry, then they cannot but be challenged. It is astonishing that, until very recently, even quite affluent congregations in the Church of England were receiving subsidies from the Church Commissioners – in the form of clergy salaries, housing and/or pensions. We have already argued that, compared with other denominations, this subsidy has tended to suppress Anglican congregational giving. However, faced with the total cost of their clergy, many congregations are now having to come to terms with the financial challenge long known to the Free Churches. It is hardly surprising if such congregations wish to have more say in the initial appointment and continuing employment of their clergy. They may become increasingly reluctant to allow central church authorities to tell them how many clergy they should have. And they are likely to demand value for money from their financial contributions supporting central church authorities. There will have to be publicly accountable checks on central costs.

Strategic church leaders, especially in the Church of England, should retain, at most, a veto over clergy appointments to self-funding churches. As already happens in a number of other parts of the Anglican Communion, local churches, provided that they are self-funding and contributing adequately to central funds, should be free to decide on how many paid clergy and laypeople they employ. They should then be free to advertise and make their own clergy appointments, as well as being encouraged to negotiate and monitor a contract of employment with their clergy once appointed. Strategic church leaders would interfere with this process as little as possible.

Instead, the function of strategic church leaders is to monitor church provision within their whole area and then identify and audit opportunities for fresh growth. We will return to this in detail in the next chapter. For the moment it is worth observing how different this style of strategic leadership is from incremental leadership. It is a bit like the difference between a poor and a good chess player. The poor player shuffles pieces around the chess board, attempting to protect them in the short-term, but with little concept of how the game will conclude. Incremental leaders tend to operate like that. Much of their time is taken up reacting to one short-term change after another. Incremental church leaders see it as their task to be instrumental in all appointments – moving clergy from one place to another. In contrast, the good chess player is concerned chiefly with long-term strategy. The strategic leader will interfere very little in day-to-day appointments, provided they fit in with the overall vision and objectives.

There is an obvious objection to self-funding churches; they become too congregational and in effect destroy the parish structure of a national church. Soon only those places which can afford to pay for stipendiary clergy and laypeople will have them. Other places, such as urban priority and deeply rural areas, will lose them altogether. As a result, all denominations will basically become suburban churches.

Victorian churches tended to solve this problem by encouraging strong congregations to build and staff mission chapels and daughter churches in poorer areas. These were the financial responsibility of the parent church and, in the case of the Church of England, tended to be looked after by curates. Gradually, however, these daughter churches were given their independence, despite the fact that many were still not self-funding. A dependent church then relied upon an unaudited central subsidy, rather than upon a locally monitored fund.

This process has created a very unhealthy situation for these dependent churches. Established in the first instance as mission experiments, they in effect became unaudited, financially dependent congregations. If strategic ownership is to be developed, it would be much better to retain them within a local relationship of budget holding. The parent and daughter church together should remain the budget holder until they are separately self-funding.

There may be no easy solution to the problems facing urban priority and deeply rural churches. However no solution at all will be found as long as they remain subsidized yet unaudited. Strategic church leadership should be bold in this area. Once unaudited subsidy is removed, then serious local initiatives can be attempted and tested. Perhaps deeply rural areas may need to rely primarily upon lay leadership, upon non-stipendiary ministry, upon a paid team ministry which is bought in as can be afforded, or upon ecumenical forms of ministry. Any of these are serious possibilities. Indeed, both of us, strongly committed to rural churches as we are, have experience of each of these solutions. However, the solution that is not sustainable is the predominant rural pattern of a heavily subsidised ministry responsible for an ever growing number of churches. Likewise in urban priority areas, much more adventurous forms of ministry can be fully explored only when unaudited, central subsidy is removed.

Strategic church leaders who break away from incremental budgeting and consensus decision making will need to operate much more like modern vice-chancellors. All too often they look more like the old-style vice-chancellors, attempting to chair large and consensus driven senates. The Church of England and a number of the Free Churches still have forms of synodical government which appear very similar to these old-style senates. Such synods are typically far too large to make effective decisions, engage in lengthy and often inconclusive debates, are enormously wasteful of members' time and resources, and expect church leaders to act as little more than 'neutral' chairs. To make matters worse, the Church of England has three layers of synodical government with no direct decision making process connecting them. Issues can be discussed at length and agreed decisively at deanery and diocesan synods and then rejected by general synod. Such a system is intended to maximize consensus, but in reality it has proved frustrating and divisive.

Once all of this is added to the dispersed nature of power in the Church of England – with the General Synod, the Church Commissioners, the Central Board of Finance, the Pensions Board, the House of Bishops and Lambeth Palace as distinct centres of authority – the problems of strategic leadership within it are only too obvious. The Turnbull Report colourfully refers to this as 'a cat's cradle of autonomous or semi-autonomous bodies with distinctive, but sometimes over-lapping, functions which are a source of confusion and wasteful duplication of effort' (para. 3.4). The Report's proposal for a National Council does go some way to resolving these problems at a national level. Unfortunately, as we have noted, it does little for the problems at synodical, diocesan or parish levels.

However, if strategic church leaders could emulate modern vice-chancellors, they too might operate on the pattern of 'top-down, bottom-up, top-down'. If they expect local con-gregations, or clusters of congregations, to be self-funding, they should allow them to make many of their own decisions. As leaders they are then free to innovate, to develop fresh strategies and to offer them as visions to their clergy and laypeople. This is the 'top-down' part of the process. It is their role as strategic leaders to do this. Congregations need then to be encouraged to share, own and develop these strategies for themselves. This is the 'bottom-up' part. Finally, church leaders need to remould their strategies in the light of the other two parts of the process and to offer clear and feasible objectives as a plan for action to be owned by all. And that, of course, is once again 'top-down'.

Of course, all of this needs to be carefully monitored. This must be our final concern.

CHAPTER EIGHT
Strategic Outcomes

When we arrived at Jerusalem, the brothers received us warmly.
The next day Paul and the rest of us went to see James and all the
elders were present. Paul greeted them and reported in detail what
God had done among the Gentiles through his ministry.

When they heard this, they praised God. Then they said to Paul:
'You see, brother, how many thousands of people have believed.'
(Acts 21.17–20)

We mentioned in the introduction that the author of Acts is
very concerned about outcomes. At several key points the
numbers of new believers are mentioned. Whereas in Paul's
letters the early Church sometimes looks beleaguered and thin
in numbers, even when quality is high, in Acts numbers
constantly grow. Of course there are set-backs. Even in Acts by
no means everyone is convinced by Peter or Paul's preaching.
Nevertheless, the author of Acts paints a broad picture of a
vibrant and growing early Church, a picture that might have
been lost if only Paul's letters had survived. Perhaps this reflects
the different perspectives of their authors or perhaps just different situations. It is, though, a useful reminder for strategic
church leadership: measuring outcomes should never be just a
matter of counting the number of churchgoers.

Churches are not petrol stations, all selling much the same
product, yet with some stations outselling others. In churches,
as indeed in universities, outcomes are rightly assessed in
qualitative as well as in quantitative terms. For both churches
and universities, quantity without quality, although it might
superficially seem exciting, is actually worthless. At the same
time, quality without quantity can be extremely depressing.
However rich in quality, a church or university which attracts
a decreasing number of people decade by decade, for over
one hundred years, has problems. A balance of quality and
quantity is the most desirable outcome.

OUTCOMES IN THE UNIVERSITIES

Agreeing on a strategic plan is exhausting, but it is only one feature of the strategic process. There is a temptation, common to all academics, to breathe a sigh of relief when a university plan is agreed and then all to go home. And who is going to put it into practice? Why the administrators of course!

That is the first mistake. Administrators are indeed essential, but they are not able to drive implementation. As we argued in the previous chapter, the institution as a whole must put its plan into practice: there must be a general sense of ownership. The second mistake is to defer the difficult decisions. This is a mistake, not only because delayed decisions often get more not less difficult, but also because delay leads to loss of the momentum that agreeing on the plan can bring. Once the endless debates and discussions have been concluded, it is the leadership's task to steer the institution forward as speedily as possible. And the third mistake is to imagine that a plan is set once for all and that the only thing remaining then is to monitor its progress year by year. On the contrary, an effective strategic process is always 'cyclical' – perhaps 'spiral' is a better model. Plans are set, tested, monitored, reviewed, adapted, set again, tested, monitored, reviewed, adapted, set . . . and so on indefinitely. Strategic leaders do need constantly to keep this process moving.

The most crucial element in all of this is the determination to make the plan work – by the whole institution, of course, but especially by the leadership. Day after day, week after week, implementation has to be driven forward. Some big decisions and hundreds of small ones – and always a tendency to delay, for all sorts of reasons. 'We don't have all the facts,' or 'Smith or Jones (one of the decision team) is away' or 'We think it's turning round, let's wait a month.' Many, many excuses to avoid making decisions. One way found useful in the University of East Anglia is never to make a decision without also deciding on the process, with firm dates attached, for implementing that decision. Another is to ask, when delay is suggested, whether all the facts that are likely to bear on the decision are available and, if they are, to insist on a decision there and then.

In addition, there are two tools that must be in place to monitor progress on a systematic base; the first financial and the second managerial.

Universities have always had to have accountable financial systems. They are responsible through their councils and the Higher Education Funding Council to Parliament, with the vice-chancellor as the accounting officer responsible to the Public Accounts Committee of the House of Commons. Nevertheless, financial systems that are fully adequate to meet the needs of external audit are often quite inadequate to deal with operational issues. Management accounts are needed for that. Businesses are accustomed to monitoring their accounts, on a monthly basis, from many areas of the company and, if necessary, rapidly adjusting. Universities too have developed such accounting systems.

For example, at the University of East Anglia, new financial systems were needed to control a mounting catering deficit. The leadership needed to know which of the many food outlets in the University were making a profit and which a loss. It was not possible to find out. Nor was it possible to adjust food prices quickly enough to reflect weekly changes in the cost of raw materials. There are other times when a university system needs to respond rapidly – for instance, when in the early 1990s the Government suddenly, in the middle of the year, reduced the amount paid per arts student. Other parts again of the university system are comparatively stable and do not need such close monitoring; salaries, for example, are only adjusted annually. The system should therefore give neither too much information nor not too little. It also goes without saying that university leaders should be able to read a financial spreadsheet.

The other essential tool is managerial; a systematic way to implement and to monitor the strategic plan. How, after the initial proposals have been adopted as objectives, and the institution has agreed a plan which will keep its expenditure inside its income, should progress be monitored? At the University of East Anglia, the major institutional objectives are turned into a series of operational objectives for each cost centre. Such operational objectives are then set for each year of the planning period, which itself is normally five years. The University has 185 operating objectives spread over 44 primary cost centres and they are all carefully reviewed, at least annually, and some more frequently. Any sign of delay in implementation or loss of direction can then be quickly corrected, either by slightly modifying objectives or by stopping the project altogether, but never by exceeding the budget. It needs constantly to be stressed that this is the University's plan, owned by all. So the question is 'How are *we* doing?' and the check-list of objectives is for everyone in the University to use. Since many of these objectives will be met on time, the process generates a sense of real progress.

It is particularly hard to bring projects to a halt, mainly because of institutional conservatism, political allegiances, or simply because people's jobs are involved. It is not just a question of closing long-running, but clearly failing, projects. It is also necessary to review, and sometimes to stop, comparatively new projects: for example those projects that are running over budget or have failed to meet key objectives. Any healthy institution should be starting new projects annually, aware that not all may work. Indeed, not all should be expected to work, for if it was certain that they would all work, then they would probably have been done years ago. Again, any healthy institution will have at least as many projects that are stopped as started. Stopping a project can be a sign not of failure but of firm and innovative leadership – firm because a decision has to be made and innovative because resources are released to try something new. Yet, since such a determined audit involves a radical change of culture, turning a conservative, consensual institution into an innovative one does not happen overnight. Such a change depends upon visionary and determined leadership.

What is true at an institutional level is also true at a personal level: it is essential to run an effective audit and appraisal system of individual performance. The two are distinct and both are necessary. Audit is a measure of performance against public, agreed criteria; it is the basis in universities for promotion or for salary increases. It is also the basis for the occasional, but necessary, action to deal with someone who is underperforming. Of course such criteria need to be as open as possible. Decisions about the performance of individuals must be publicly defensible if personal bias and prejudice are to be avoided. However difficult it is to write clear, unambiguous criteria for such professionals as university lecturers or parish priests, it does need to be done. A number of recent cases of malpractice in both universities and churches show the clear need for this.

Appraisal is quite different; it is private rather than public, and it is concerned with personal objectives. In universities, it now commonly involves an annual review, lasting at least an hour, with a more senior member of staff in which objectives set a year ago are reviewed against progress, and new objectives are set. In the universities, as distinct from the civil service and many businesses, it is not linked to salaries, although helpful appraisal and successful attainment of objectives obviously will help when salaries are considered. However, the two processes are separate, and appraisal is a totally confidential way of measuring progress and identifying, and seeking to eliminate, barriers to that progress. There are many kinds of barriers; personal problems, difficult interpersonal relationships, an unreasonable manager, a need for training and many others. It is the responsibility of the appraiser to find ways to deal with the problems. Then people can really be helped to do better. Encouragement is rarely sufficient; problems do have to be resolved. Such a system of appraisal is beginning to be established for clergy too. This is a welcome, even if strictly limited, innovation.

OUTCOMES IN THE CHURCHES

In the previous chapter we argued that strategic church leaders should encourage self-funding churches or clusters of churches and should adopt a 'top-down, bottom-up, top-down' style of decision making. At first sight this might seem to do them out of a job altogether. Self-funding churches would finance, appoint and monitor their own paid clergy and layworkers, alongside their unpaid ministry. They would also join wholeheartedly in the process of central decision making. In turn, church leaders would lose much of their patronage and power of appointment. Would there be anything left for church leaders to do?

Indeed there would be. There has recently been a radical shift of understanding about leaders in organizations. Church leaders might learn much from this. Peter Senge expresses the shift as follows:

> Our traditional view of leaders – as special people who set the direction, make the key decisions, and energize the troops

– are deeply rooted in an individualistic and nonsystematic worldview. Especially in the West, leaders are *heroes* – great men (and occasionally women) who 'rise to the fore' in times of crisis. Our prevailing leadership myths are still captured by the image of the captain of the cavalry leading the charge to rescue the settlers from the attacking Indians . . . The new view of leadership in learning organizations centers on subtler and more important tasks. In a learning organization, leaders are designers, stewards and teachers. They are responsible for *building organizations* where people continually expand their capabilities to understand complexity, clarify vision, and improve shared mental models – that is, they are responsible for learning. (*The Fifth Discipline*, Century Business, 1992, p. 340)

On this new understanding, church leaders would be free to provide and foster vision – theological, moral and strategic – and to enable this vision to be realized by the whole church. It would be their job as strategic leaders to think, to plan prayerfully, to coax, to monitor, to help others to learn, and, above all, to identify and enhance opportunities for qualitative and quantitative growth and to be firm about subsidized projects that do not promote growth. Only by carefully monitoring outcomes, both quantitatively and qualitatively, would they be able to do this job effectively.

After the public debate about the Church Commissioners' investment losses it is not surprising that the Turnbull Report sees a clear need for audit in this specific area. It proposes that the Commissioners, after being much slimmed down, should lose their function of allocating central income. Instead the Commissioners will remain only managers and trustees of the historic central assets of the Church of England. There is some irony in this, since it was this role which they did so badly in the 1980s. Even their published investment accounts in the 1990s remain less than pellucid. However, the Report argues that this whole process must now be properly audited:

An Audit Committee would, with the assistance of the Commissioners' external auditors, scrutinise annually all aspects of the work of the Commissioners. The Comptroller and Auditor or any appointed firm of independent auditors would continue to report on the accounts of the

Commissioners before they were laid before Parliament. (8.22)

So far so good. What the Turnbull Report does not do is suggest how audit should be extended to a diocesan and then to parish level. Simply auditing resources at a national level is insufficient. If money is raised through the prudent investments of the restructured Church Commissioners and then distributed to dioceses by the new National Council, its subsequent use does need to be audited. More specifically, it is essential that the National Council must be given an annual audit of how these distributed resources to dioceses are being used for mission. Dioceses would be required to make bids for these resources to meet specific objectives agreed with the National Council before any money was released. They would then have to show the National Council that these objectives had been met before receiving further funds in future years. Only on this basis could the National Council know if its resources were being used strategically in a way that fits its own mission objectives. Strategic church leadership demands nothing less than public accountability.

To return once again to our own mission statement:

The central aim of churches in modern Britain is the communal worship of God in Christ through the Spirit, teaching and moulding as many lives and structures as deeply as possible through this worship.

In the light of this mission statement, a central aim of church leaders should be to promote Christian worship and to enable as many people as possible to take part in this worship. Strategic church leaders should be engaged in a continuous attempt to promote this aim – seeking to identify those areas where it is realized as well as those where it is not. They will need to undertake a considerable amount of analysis of each congregation in their care, to monitor innovations and sometimes to make tough decisions about subsidies to existing structures.

For example, supposing it is found, as a result of careful analysis, that a number of church buildings in city-centre or deeply rural areas contribute little to the overall numbers of those who worship in an area. However, the church buildings involved are mostly magnificent, hallowed by history and contributing much to the wonders of architecture. How can church leaders possibly decide to withdraw a subsidy from them? There will be enormous pressure to preserve these buildings as a part of the 'rich heritage' of the church and nation – as was seen in the decision in the Diocese of London not to act on the recommendations of the Templeman Commission to close City churches. Yet, in terms of our mission statement, strategic church leaders must surely decide otherwise. Their priority is clear. Looking after magnificent historic buildings for their own sake is not a central aim of the churches. The *raison d'être* of church buildings is to provide places for Christian worship.

Stated as bluntly as that such a policy may seem too harsh. Several counter arguments will usually be made. First, it should not be assumed that existing populations will remain static. There may eventually be a significant return of populations to deeply rural and even to city-centre areas. A prudent church, so it will be argued, will maintain its historic buildings for such an eventuality. Second, city-centre churches may take on additional functions in the absence of a resident population. For example, they could become venues for office workers to use in the day-time, for recreational and sometimes for spiritual purposes. Third, resources from the past were often donated to maintain such buildings: it would be wrong for central church authorities to use these resources for other purposes.

A strategic response to these counter arguments could be as follows:

If churches are indeed self-funding, in both maintenance and ministry, then they can be free to perform a number of functions, provided of course that Christian worship is still at their centre. If they are subsidized, then strategic church leaders should always ask searching questions about the value of this particular subsidy alongside other claims on the resources involved. So, having heard arguments about possible future movements of population and the recreational function of city-centre churches, if church leaders find that other claims better meet the agreed mission statement, then it is the latter that should be preferred. Strategic church leaders should be prepared to face considerable criticism – from the heritage lobby, from politicians, from influential laypeople, from the media –

insisting that church resources ought primarily to be used for fostering worship amongst the living. They might even point out that many Victorians, who left considerable endowments to maintain church buildings, shared this priority. Victorians were overwhelmingly concerned to provide places for people to worship rather than historic buildings in areas devoid of effective populations. They were usually far more radical in assessing building needs for worship than many churches are today.

Of course church leaders should not just abandon all city-centre and rural churches. Rather it is a question of priorities and main objectives. Once they are clear about these, then strategic church leaders will be in a better position to assess which buildings should be retained for worship and which should be preserved instead by others. Perhaps it will be English Heritage which maintains this second group of buildings, or perhaps it is local patrons or trusts. Perhaps some buildings would be better preserved as private housing. There are an increasing number of secular solutions being found for those church buildings which are no longer needed for worship. Whatever solutions are adopted, strategic church leaders will be clear that maintaining historic buildings for their own sake is not a central aim of the churches

Strategic church leaders will spend a great deal of time and energy experimenting, encouraging innovations and carefully monitoring new ventures for signs of qualitative and quantitative growth. They will realize that growth in any institution requires careful and, for churches, prayerful planning. There is a curious myth which suggests that British church growth in the first half of the nineteenth century happened spontaneously. We argued earlier that in fact Victorian churches showed an enormous amount of energy and imagination based upon a renewed theological commitment. Across denominations they built daughter churches, chapels and church schools. Anglicans founded new dioceses and restored many ancient parish churches. The sheer energy of early Victorian churches should not be underestimated. And many local congregations buzzed with activity throughout the week – with choirs, clubs, fellowships and philanthropic works. Planning, intelligence, imagination and energy are all essential if denominations are once more to grow.

Robin Gill has already set out in earlier books many of the structural ways that churches might grow – at parish level in *Beyond Decline* (1988) and *A Vision for Growth* (1994) and at a statistical and structural level in *The Myth of the Empty Church* (1993) – so it is not necessary to repeat them all here. Our focus is more limited. There is abundant evidence that, despite the ambivalence of much modern culture to Christianity, churches can achieve modest growth if their leaders have sufficient vision, boldness and energy.

Just two examples might be given – the one sometimes requiring an economic subsidy and the other not.

To take the one which requires no subsidy first, there is strong evidence that small, supportive groups are an essential feature of many growing churches. A study done recently in the United States suggests that such groups in congregations are highly effective in changing people's views and behaviour. Belonging to such a group is more influential than regular churchgoing or even than the orthodoxy of an individual's Christian beliefs. People who worship in small groups become significantly more likely than those who do not to give their time and money both to church activities and to voluntary care in the community. In Britain it also seems that church groups are highly influential both in church planting and in encouraging outsiders to join more fully in church life.

Fostering such groups could become a key role for strategic church leaders. Renewal movements within churches are best achieved, not through large rallies (they have their place but it can be greatly exaggerated), but through well-organized and committed groups. An excellent use of church leaders' time is to let them move from one group to another – stimulating, inspiring, coaxing, comparing, re-invigorating. The tendency of too many church leaders is to spend a great deal of their time instead making appointments, chairing committees, and meeting church groups to resolve one problem or another. Strategic leaders might decide to delegate many of these functions to others and devote a significant amount of their time to visiting groups amongst the churches in their care.

The other example may sometimes require a judicious use of subsidy. There are many urban and suburban areas that are ripe for the development of more effective family worship. Given an area with a sufficient number of those young parents who still see the need for worship and for passing on Christian values to their children in a confusing world, imaginative family services can attract sizeable congregations. As we noted earlier, growing congregations often decide to hire school halls for these services, sometimes, but certainly not always, as a prelude to a church plant. In other congregations a new family service is established alongside existing services in a church.

A strategic church leader would not simply encourage such developments, but might also provide them with an initial, albeit carefully monitored, subsidy. Herein lies a major trap. The temptation of the Church of England, in the 1950s especially, has been to subsidize churches in urban priority areas and on new housing estates and then to continue this subsidy indefinitely. Frequently the subsidy has taken the form of providing a church building financed almost entirely from outside the area. Routinely it has also taken the form of providing salaried clergy to work in these areas, with little or no expectation that their congregations would ever become self-funding. In contrast, the Roman Catholic Church and Afro-Caribbean Churches – lacking the historic resources of the Church Commissioners – have tended to work, rather more successfully, in urban priority areas relying upon finances raised locally.

If strategic leaders provide subsidies for mission, these subsidies should be time limited and carefully monitored. Proposers of any project should realize at the outset that they are not being granted an indefinite subsidy. At most, they are being given temporary resources to allow a particular project to get started. Once started a project must establish a form of ministry that a congregation can sustain for itself. Perhaps, in this respect, the losses of the Church Commissioners will be a blessing in disguise for Anglicans. Before the investment losses it seldom seemed necessary to question subsidies to churches. However, if central subsidies are derived not from inherited resources, but from top-slicing parish quotas to central funds, churches have every reason to monitor these subsidies carefully and prudently. Audited, time limited subsidies derived from top-slicing could become very powerful means of achieving mission. If after five years it was discovered that a subsidized project had achieved no discernible qualitative or quantitative growth, then the funds involved would be given instead to a more promising project.

By now the main role of strategic church leadership should be clear. Strategic church leaders constantly send out experimental feelers, encouraging innovations and probes to see where there might be opportunities for growth. Such leaders realize that many of these probes will eventually prove fruitless and will then need to be replaced by others. Increasingly, it is recognized that a variety of experiments which fail (as well as some which succeed) is actually a sign that an organization is healthy. Growing churches should expect to have plenty of failures: it is declining churches which take no risks. By monitoring carefully, prayerfully and truthfully the effectiveness of any particular probe, church leaders might discern which is a genuine opportunity for growth and which is not.

The Church of Scotland offers a fascinating example of a church that has been more rigorous than most but which has finally neglected this central function of strategic innovation. As a result of its reunion in 1929 with the United Free Church, it has been faced with a huge structural problem of duplicate church buildings throughout Scotland. It has rigorously closed churches, amalgamated charges (more than halving them over the years) and required most churches to be self-supporting. Although these measures have helped to keep the Church of Scotland stronger than the Church of England, they have not stanched its decline. Communicant membership in 1929 amounted to over a third of the adult population of Scotland, whereas today it amounts to less than a fifth. More significantly still, this is a church which now loses twice as many members (through death or removal) as it gains, whereas in 1929 its gains slightly outnumbered its losses. Lacking an effective leadership it has found central, strategic planning for growth exceedingly difficult.

Strategic church leaders should treat outcomes as a vital tool of accountable leadership. Of course, all of the features of leadership that we have sketched in this book are interrelated. Outcomes come last in our analysis, yet emphatically they are not the end. Effective leadership is concerned about outcomes, but it also keeps returning to all of the other features. Outcomes are but a stage – albeit a vital and sometimes neglected stage – in the whole process of strategic leadership. Used wisely outcomes allow strategic church leaders to discern which innovations meet their mission criteria and which do not. The latter must be courteously discontinued: the former need to be fostered and copied elsewhere. To achieve this, church leaders need to be both tough and wise . . . exactly like Paul in Acts.

INDEX

accountability 2, 10, 36, 70, 81f.
Acts of the Apostles 3, 4f., 12, 25, 37, 41, 47, 50–2, 60, 62, 65, 71, 74, 75–6, 81, 93
Allen, Roland 33–4
Alternative Service Book 57
appointments 77f.
Anglican Communion, The 58, 77
appraisal 42, 85
Archbishop of Canterbury 35, 41, 56
audit 41, 83f.

Book of Common Prayer 57
budgets 26f., 63f., 68–70, 72, 75

change (social/political/eco-nomical) 12f., 37, 44
church buildings, redundancy of 88f.
Church Commissioners 1, 20, 32f., 43, 59, 77, 86–7, 91
church finances 31f., 43
churchgoing 30f., 46f., 55
Church of England 54f., 77f.
Church of Scotland 54, 92
church planting 70
clergy appointments 77f.
conflict 7–10, 65–6
consensus 1, 10, 68, 73, 79

Decade of Evangelism 39, 52–3
delayering, of jobs 16

East Anglia University 26f., 60f., 73, 82–3
employment 16f., 26f., 37
Evangelical Churches 31

Faith in the City 52
financial control, in universi-ties 83
Free Churches 30f., 40, 42, 77, 79

growth, of churches 89f.

Handy, Charles 16–17, 24
Higher Education Funding Council 83
House of Commons Social Security Committee 34–6, 43

inclusiveness 57
incremental budgeting 68, 72
information technology 18

Jews, corporate worship 47

Kemp, Bishop Eric 39

Index

managerialism 41
marginalization of church 56
McCulloch, Bishop Nigel
39–40, 42
Methodist Church 68
ministry 40, 42, 77f.
Mintzberg, Henry 40, 42
mission statement 44f., 49, 69,
87
Moore, Peter 16
Muslims, corporate worship
47
Myth of the Empty Church 30, 90

National Health Service 2,
17, 20, 26, 38

objectives 54, 61, 71, 83–4;
appraisal of 85
opportunities 6, 50f.
outcomes 10, 69, 81f.
ownership 2, 7, 9, 71f.

parochial system 56
pastoral committees 67
Paul 4f., 25, 35, 37, 50–2, 60,
62, 65, 71, 81, 93
pensions 34f., 76
Peter 4f., 75, 81
politics 13f.
priorities 2, 6, 37f., 61f., 71

research 38
resource allocation 61, 63
Roman Catholic Church 30f.,
57, 67

Sanhedrin 8
savings 62

secularism 58
Senge, Peter 85–6
service 48
spiritual directors 40–1
strategic leadership 1, 4f., 9,
11, 12f., 28, 38f., 63, 73,
77f., 82, 89f.
strategic planning 40f., 60f.,
82f.
strengths 53f.
subsidy 35, 43, 59, 77f., 88,
90
Sunday School Worship
45–6
SWOT analysis 52f., 73
synodical government 79–80

Templeman Commission 88
theological agenda 41f., 86
threats, to church stability 6,
50f.
Turnbull Report 2, 12, 20, 31,
33, 39, 41, 48–9, 59, 67–8,
76, 80, 86–7

universities 20f., 25f., 53, 60f.,
71f., 82f.
University Grants Committee
64
United Free Church 92

vision 5, 44, 71, 75, 86

weaknesses 53f.
witness 48
World Council of Churches
47
worship 5, 45f., 70, 90